Contents

A tap water girl in a
bottled water world

Reflections on belonging and believing

For Odis –
May these stories fill
your heart spaces the
way you filled heart
spaces. I grateful
for your friendship!

Warmly,

Everything that happens to you is your teacher. The secret is to learn to sit at the feet of your own life and be taught by it.

— Polly B. Berends

With an overflowing heart, I dedicate this book to my families.

To my first family: Mary, Bobby, and Ricky—who held hands with me during the toughest times.

To my forever family: Mama and Daddy (the late Winnie and Aubrie Duncan), Lamar, and Mary. And the Gillhams and the Duncans who loved me as one of their own. They encouraged me to be a tap water girl and anything else I wanted to be.

And to my newest family: Randy, my husband, and the family he has shared with me—children, grandchildren, Garretts, Roops, and Heards.

This book is also dedicated to *all* families who sing in the car.

A tap water girl in a
bottled water world

Reflections on belonging and believing

PROLOGUE

Dippity Doo Da! Dippity Day!

It was 1967 and I had all the tools for success: Lady Clairol electric rollers (hot and ready to go), a can of Final Net hair spray (extra hold), and a jar of Dippity Doo. I was a junior in high school and my success, self-esteem, and hope for the day all centered around one thing—a hairdo with a great flip—because that's what Nancy Malone had. And my goal was to look just like Nancy Malone. Truth be told, not only did I want to look like Nancy, I wanted to be Nancy.

She had it all. Dark hair that flipped out on its own and olive skin graced by just enough freckles to make you smile. Her body was cheerleader perfect. And she made good grades to boot. Nancy was on the homecoming court and dated the star football player.

I wanted to hate her. But Nancy had something that made me really like her. She had that personality trait that always seemed to elude me. She was confident. She was sure of herself without being cocky. She was friendly to everyone. She was comfortable. She seemed to like who she was.

Oh, how I envied Nancy, yet throughout high school I

always tried to position myself close enough to her to experience her confidence. I yearned for that someday when whatever she had would rub off on me. My high school years were hard. I was challenged daily to have a certain look, wear a certain label, make certain grades, and most of all, to be liked by certain people.

When I went away to college, I realized that I would never become Nancy Malone. So I settled for being someone else— Farrah Fawcett.

College was another emotionally turbulent (as well as exciting) time. I took on one role model after another, thinking that each new heroine would help me become the person I wanted to be. It was not until I was in my thirties that I discovered a truth that would help me embrace the life I was destined to lead.

Here's how the truth was revealed to me: I overheard a friend describe a local eccentric woman called Lydia. The discussion focused on a social event, and a bit of harmless gossip about something Lydia did at the event. Not knowing Lydia, I asked about her: "Where does she live? Who is she married to? What does she do?" Without skipping a beat, my friend replied, "Oh, it's a full-time job just being Lydia."

In that moment, I realized my own truth. It is a full-time job just being me—and that is enough!

Now at mid-life, I have other insights. I'm probably never going to be a Rockette; I won't be the anchor of the *Today Show* nor the first woman on the moon. Someone else will receive the Nobel Prize for curing breast cancer, and my grandsons will probably not grow up to be President. I may or may not write the great American novel, and I'll never make the cover of Martha Stewart's *Living* magazine.

What I will do is enjoy this rather bizarre, yet comforting, life that is mine. I will acknowledge who I am and who I am not. I will open myself to friendship. I will open my home to friends. I will walk to raise money for a cure. And I will sit up late at night watching old movies with my grandchildren. I will open my heart to people who are hurting. And I will open my mind to those who are different. I will laugh a lot, cry a little. I will be proud. And I will be disappointed. I will be mischievous and I will be pensive. I will be who I was intended to be—a tap-water girl in a bottled-water world!

It has been quite a journey just to get to this point, and these stories chronicle my path. When I began to write, I thought I was writing humorous, anecdotal tales of my life experiences. As I progressed, though, I realized that these stories are about something else, something more. When I share stories written for this book, people often exclaim to me, "Oh that happened to me, too!" Or they say, "I felt exactly that same way!"

I realize these stories are about experiences that are universal. They are about growing up and finding out what really matters. And they are about learning what we need to know from the people we encounter during our lives. They are stories about the discovery of self.

As you read about some of my growing experiences, you will meet some of the people who held my hand or gave me an emotional boost or taught me a life lesson. But more importantly, I hope you will recognize bits and pieces of your own journey and the people who held your hand along the way. And perhaps this book will serve as a mirror for you to reflect on, see the wonder, and embrace the essence of your own life.

Tuning Out, Tuning In

I was four years old the last time I saw my birth mother. She came to the orphanage to visit her children—me, my little sister Mary, and our older brothers Bobby and Ricky. We had been taken away from her.

I remember my birth mother as beautiful, breathy, and always in some kind of hurry. That last day, she wore a long coat with a red scarf and pretty, high-heeled shoes. I don't remember what we did during her visit, but I can never forget her leaving. I stood watching as she walked down the long hallway, her high-heeled shoes clicking on the tile floor with each step. My arms were outstretched, I cried out for her to stop. I wanted one more kiss, one more hug.

Like time frozen in a movie frame, I can still replay the moment she abruptly turned around, and without a change in expression, quickly blew a kiss from her lips. Just as quickly, she turned and walked away.

That was one of the few days I remember from the months at the orphanage. The rest are blurred with only a couple of events separating one day from another. But my memory is full of the events that led up to my life in the orphanage.

My birth mother was from Germany and had married our father when he was stationed in the United States Army overseas. Our family was living in Atlanta near an Army base, but our father was gone most of the time.

Our birth mother didn't do a very good job of being a mama. I think it was hard for her to look after her four children, ages two through six. Maybe it was because she had been born in Germany, spoke with a heavy accent, and was new to the United States. Or maybe it was because she didn't have any family or girlfriends to help.

Maybe what she really needed was a husband around to help her take care of their four stair-step children. When our Army father did come home, she was probably exhausted and frustrated. I still remember hiding under the covers of my bed and listening to them yell at each other.

One time I even heard the sound of furniture being shoved around, and the next morning there was a hole in the wall exactly the same size as the picture tube that protruded from the back of the television set. That is not a good memory.

After that incident, it seemed that life got more uncertain for my siblings and me. Our father took us away from our house and our mother. He took us to live with his sister, our aunt, and her husband for a while. I did not like my aunt or her house very much.

Before the move, we had lived in a small, white frame house in Atlanta. There were lots of neighbors close by and yards with grass for playing. But our aunt's house was out in the country and sat off a dirt road. The house was unpainted inside and out, and balanced atop wobbly looking piles of rocks. I thought it was strange that we could see under the house all the way from one side to the other. Later I learned that the underpinning was missing. Houses like this one were known as tenant houses. The yard was a flat piece of untended, red, Georgia clay—dusty, dirty, and uninviting. Not nearly as inviting as the grassy backyard at our other house, the house where our mother and father lived (at least I thought our father still lived there when he was not in the Army).

Our uncle worked on the night shift, which meant he had to sleep all day. So on some days, we four noisy children were locked out of the house.

One day we were put outside kind of early—and without breakfast. Baby, our pet name for Sister Mary, was hungry and needed something to eat. So the brothers, Mary, and I walked down the road, past a row of mailboxes, and all the way to a neighbor's house. My next memory is of a screened door opening, seeing the face of a woman, and standing in her yard eating dry cereal out of the box.

It may have been the begging incident or the living situation, but for whatever reason, the living arrangement with the aunt and uncle didn't work out either.

That is how I found myself in a great big building called an orphanage, still trying to figure out how to look after Baby. I wanted to make things right for her, but how could I, when I wasn't even sure where we were or why we were there?

What I did know was that this place was too big and too scary. The grown-up people in charge didn't understand why I felt it was my job to look after my little sister. I understood better than they that Baby was only a two-year-old who didn't have a mother anymore, or a father. During the first day at the orphanage, the ladies who said they were going to help us wanted to take Baby to another room—one upstairs where they said they had cribs and she would sleep more safely.

I wasn't about to fall for that, I was not going to let Baby out of my sight! I was going to stay right by the side of her crib—if I could just find it. I don't know if I cried, or begged, or sat in defiant silence. I don't remember. I just know that I stayed close. That is, until one of the ladies mentioned a nap. While I hated taking naps myself, I finally agreed to let go of Baby so she could sleep. I decided to wait right where I was until she woke up and they brought her back.

In an attempt to lure me away from Baby, someone took my hand and led me down a long hall to show me a playground through the window. No matter how much fun the other children were having on the swings and in the sandbox, I knew I could not go outside and be further away from my little sister.

She was somewhere in the front of the building—upstairs. What if she awakened? What if she needed me? What if she discovered that we didn't have a mother, father, or even a mean aunt to look after us anymore? What if she was scared? What kind of big sister would go play when Baby might need her?

Instead, I remember looking sadly out the window, determined not to let the laughter of the other children entice me to join the fun—not during such a frightful time for Baby. Standing there, watching my breath cloud the window, I willed myself not to yield to the temptation to go outside.

I saw my brothers playing outside. After all, they were boys, they were older, and they had each other. I was the one who had to be close at hand for Baby.

As that first day and then evening wore on, a compassionate adult staff member found me lying in my little single bed with my eyes wide open. That same person carried me upstairs to a cot to sleep in the room with Mary. Whoever moved me had made an attempt to right my very topsy-turvy world. What a relief!

The months at the orphanage were strange but uneventful until the last day our mother visited. Something she said, I don't remember what, made me think that it was not right that we lived in an orphanage. We didn't belong there.

Not long after the final good-bye kiss from our mother, things began to change. We kept hearing the word *adoption* and tried to understand just what it meant. I knew it had something to do with a new mama, a new daddy, a new brother, and ice cream. And I knew that Baby and I would get to sleep in the same room forever!

I also learned that it had something to do with Bobby and Ricky getting a different mama and daddy. But we would live close enough to each other to play together. And Bobby would stay with Mary and me during the day while our new parents taught school. Ricky was six years old and he was going to go to school. Mary and I were going to get another brother named Lamar. He was a teenager and was the natural son of our new Mama and Daddy. Mary and I didn't know what a teenager or a natural son was, but we were excited to have one more brother.

Bobby, Ricky, Mary, and I left the orphanage together. In order for us to all fit into one car, only the two new mamas drove to the orphanage to take us to our new houses. When we got to the small rural town of Jackson, Georgia, all of us would meet our new daddies. Later I learned that, when people asked our new daddy how he could adopt two little girls, sight unseen, he replied, "It doesn't matter what they look like; if they need a home, we want them."

During the drive to our new homes, our first stop was for ice cream. So far, adoption was pretty good and looking even better. But then I got worried. I didn't want to do something bad and get us all in trouble. I didn't want to mess things up for Baby or Bobby or Ricky—or me! I was wearing a brand-new dress with a pretty white collar, and when the first drop of chocolate ice cream fell onto the collar, I burst into tears. I was sure my new mama was going to send me back to the orphanage. Imagine my surprise when she said, "It's okay, baby doll. We'll just wash it out when we get home!" I didn't know what *baby doll* meant, but I knew it felt good to be called one.

As we rode along the country roads, our new mamas started singing to us. They sang *Jesus Loves Me, God Bless America, I'm a Little Teapot,* and finally, *Jesus Loves the Little Children.* How I loved the words to that song, ". . . all the children of the world. Red and yellow, black and white, they are precious in His sight. Jesus loves the little children of the world."

As we drove into the front yard of our new house, the two new Daddies were sitting on the porch waiting for us. Lamar was pitching a baseball against the side of the house and catching it. For the first time in a very long time, I believed that life would be happy. Maybe I could let go of taking care of Mary. Maybe we were going to be safe. And even though we would not be living with our brothers, maybe we would be a family.

Little did I know that a new family tradition was born that day. Mama continued to sing, teaching us the words so we could all join in. We sang wonderful songs about teapots and Bill Groggins' Goat. We sang patriotic songs about amber waves of grain and the rocket's red glare. We sang songs about amazing grace and when the roll is called up yonder (wherever yonder was). We sang songs that required hand motions and we sang songs in rounds. We sang wonderfully fun songs, full of life and joy—*My Grandfather's Clock, Oh Suzanna* and *My Bonnie Lies Over the Ocean.* And we always sang "Jesus loves the little children, all the children of the world."

We loved being part of this new family. We went to Sunday School and church. We took vacations and went to family reunions. No matter where we went, we sang songs. We sang as we traveled the long, hot hours to our summer vacation in Florida. We sang as we crossed the back roads of Georgia to visit all the aunts and uncles and cousins that came along with our new family. We sang on the way to watch high school basketball games—and since our new Daddy was the high school principal and Lamar played ball, we made a lot of these trips.

Mama would tease Daddy about being off-key. We certainly didn't mind that he couldn't find the key, and he didn't seem to mind the teasing. Daddy often made us laugh even harder by making up funny ad-lib words to the songs. We were even more delighted that finally there was something to sing about. A family to love and to be loved by. Lessons to learn and life to experience. I knew that something good had happened in spite of a very rough beginning.

Almost 45 years after joining our new family, as Mary and I were "breaking up housekeeping" for Mama, I found an old, old songbook among the numerous books she had collected during the years, *Songs for All: A Collection of Favorite Songs*, published in 1935. As I flipped through the pages of the familiar titles, I could still hear a family—my family—singing from the top of our lungs and the bottom of our hearts.

The sounds of the high-heeled shoes, an unkind aunt, and an orphanage are now very far away. I can barely hear them at all over the laughter and songs from the back seat of a two-toned blue 1955 Dodge that carried a family—a real family—to ball games and reunions, vacation and church, and then back home again.

Daddy's Gift

One Christmas, not long ago, I was worn out. All the holiday activities were draining. I felt depleted of energy, enthusiasm, and the confidence to get it all done. Looking for a way to leave the Christmas commotion behind, I wandered outdoors and straddled my bicycle. It's a regular old bicycle, nothing fancy, but just the right vehicle to free my spirit. As I pedaled up the driveway toward the street, I was reminded of my favorite family story—one I've heard countless times over the past years. One that's told at every family gathering without fail. Gathering speed, trees blurring as I passed, I replayed the story once again in my mind.

It was just a month before Christmas 1955 when Mary and I moved into our new home, and those first weeks with Daddy, Mama, and Lamar were joyful, but emotionally (if not actually) expensive. We brought with us a lot of needs: tonsils that needed removing, prescriptions that needed to be filled, and clothes that needed to be bought (we had come from the orphanage with only one change of clothes). But our greatest need was for emotional support and reassurance that this was indeed our home—for life.

As small-town people often do, the community pitched in: neighbors hosted a children's shower, the local pharmacist donated the needed medications, and someone even provided a new tricycle for Santa to bring Mary for Christmas.

Mary and I were so excited about Christmas. We had learned about Jesus and how much he loved us. For the first time in our lives, we listened to Bible stories, learned the words to "Jesus Loves Me," asked the blessing, and said our prayers. For the very first time, we understood that Christmas was about Baby Jesus.

Mary and I also discovered that Christmas was about presents! As the holidays approached, Aunt Florice, one of Daddy's sisters, was secretly putting the finishing touches on three matching mother-daughter dresses. Daddy knew the surprise would leave Mama in tears. Lamar was old enough to help plan the details of how Santa would deliver the rest of the presents. There were new baby dolls, building blocks that had been made in the shop from leftover bits of wood, and special stocking stuffers. Everything seemed to be in order for the wonderful Christmas celebration—yet Daddy was restless. He couldn't forget about the small blue bicycle "Santa" could buy for ten dollars. He and Mama agreed they had spent enough for the time being. After all, there was always the chance our birth parents would reclaim us—a right they could exercise for up to a year.

On Christmas Eve, Daddy paced and thought—and thought and paced. He knew that I wore the most profound scars of our past. I was afraid of the dark, afraid of enclosed spaces, afraid to even go to the bathroom alone. In fact, I could not speak an intelligible sentence and often they needed little Mary to interpret for me!

As dusk began to fall, he told Mama he had one last errand to run. Many years later I learned that when Daddy returned with the bicycle (complete with training wheels), he declared, "Heck, if they take Shirley back, they can just take the bicycle too!"

On Christmas morning, my eyes grew wide as I saw the beautiful blue bicycle beside the tree. I couldn't wait to take it outside to the sidewalk. Daddy was eager to help me learn and he quickly recognized that I didn't need the training wheels after all. When they were removed, I began to pedal and Daddy released his hold on the bicycle, sending me off for the first time on the road to freedom. But even as he let me go, he ran alongside. He was there to help me if I wavered too far off course. He was always like that.

Recalling this story in 2000, I continued to ride, but now I had a renewed spirit about the holiday season. Calmed and recharged, I realized that first bike ride had been the beginning of what would be a lifetime of send-offs. And with each one—whether I was attending my first day of school, learning to drive a car, heading off to college, or searching for my first real job—that is how Daddy parented. He always provided me with a way to soar and with the training wheels of a stable home for balance. Daddy's parental love and guidance were always there beside me, ready to support and redirect me if needed.

As I rode along, a melody began playing in my head and I entered a straight-a-way. Suddenly, the knowledge of unconditional love filled me with confidence. I rediscovered my center of balance, released the handlebars, and lifted my hands to the sky in jubilant celebration and gratefulness for Daddy's gift.

Every Kid Needs a Butler

Crawling, walking, talking, reading. Natural progression. Kids do it all the time. It is the order of life and learning, usually.

About a year after our adoption, we moved to Butler, another rural Georgia town. Daddy became the principal of a school system that allowed us to live closer to his family home. For a few weeks, we lived in a tiny house until a bigger house around the corner was ready for us.

The big house in Butler (as we always called it) was typical of many homes of its era. The front door opened off the wraparound front porch into a wide hallway. Large rooms were on each side of the hallway and the kitchen was at the back.

The telephone table and phone were in the hallway. Mary and I spent a lot of time there while Mama talked on the telephone. She sat at the little table talking with Miss Nellie or Miss Inez—discussing school, church, canasta parties, or other such wonderful grown-up stuff. Mary and I sat just out of her reach and mimicked everything she said. Mama would look at us over the rim of her glasses with a stare that meant business.

We never got too worried, though, until she started snapping her thumb and middle finger, followed immediately by a stern pointing of the index finger. We would debate whether to give up the game and get out of sight while there was still a chance, or push it to the edge. Mary and I had a knack for pushing it to the edge.

Inevitably, Mama would finally hang up the phone and the lecture would start. Try as we might, Mary and I could not suppress our laughter, and on lucky days, Mama would give up and laugh with us. On less lucky days, we received a popping on our backsides and quickly got out of her way.

It was in the big house in Butler that I watched the *Little Rascals* and *Zorro* on the television in Mama and Daddy's room. It was just off the kitchen and was large enough to double as the family room. The real living room was saved for company.

When I was sick with the measles, I got to stay in Mama and Daddy's room. I spent the day in their double bed—all the shades pulled so the sun wouldn't hurt my eyes. After I milked the measles for all they were worth, I moved back into the room behind the kitchen that Mary and I shared.

The big house in Butler was extra special because that is where I learned to read—and to speak clearly. When Mary and I were adopted, it was almost impossible for people outside our family to understand me. Mama was sensitive enough to realize that the problem was not due to lack of intellect, but a combination of my fear, neglect, and perhaps a melding of two languages, English and German.

One very special summer day, Mama set up a card table in Lamar's big bedroom. His room was just off the hallway, across from the telephone table, and it had lots of sunlight. She invited me to sit across from her as she opened a mysterious box. It was oddly shaped—more narrow than a shoebox, but about the same height and depth. The box was filled from end to end with little cards. Something was written on both sides, something that I was sure would make sense someday.

There we began: "a, e, i, o, u"—long a, short a—big A, little a. And it wasn't too long before Dick, Jane, Spot, and Tag became a part of our special hour. It was marvelous! I was learning to speak and to correctly pronounce my vowels, consonants, and blends. (Years later, when I picked up school slang and a more pronounced Southern dialect, Mama would say," I don't know what happened! When Shirley was five years old, she could enunciate perfectly.") It was a glorious time for me! I was speaking in a voice that other people could understand. Mary no longer had to interpret for me. I could express myself!

Oh, that house in Butler was the background for a lot of other treasured memories. Mary and I started digging our first "hole to China" in the side yard. We discovered the mystery of pregnancy as we discussed the relationship between the fat tummies of neighborhood women and new babies. After watching new mamas nurse their babies, we held our own baby dolls close to our breasts. We carefully covered ourselves and our baby dolls with a blanket, but couldn't figure out what all the *hush, hush* was about.

In our backyard, there was a huge tree with branches low enough and strong enough for us to climb. It was there that I began discovering both my tomboy self and my love for solitude in nature. Near the garage, Daddy planted a family garden where he liked to putter. Close by, Mary and I had our very own sandbox. We would while away the hot, muggy afternoons of middle Georgia playing, climbing, and pretending in the back yard.

In the fall of the second year in Butler, my world expanded even more. I started first grade and began to understand what girlfriends and secrets were all about. I learned to jump rope and even how to "run in" while the rope was turning. Just after school started, I celebrated my sixth birthday with my first real birthday party. The celebration took place in the back yard, at a picnic table by the sandbox. I loved being the center of attention for the day, but I loved my bride doll even more. She was the most beautiful bride doll in the world and I knew that one day I would get to look just like her!

Lamar was in high school and played on the basketball team. Mary and I were mascot cheerleaders so we jumped and yelled alongside the high school girls in our very own miniature outfits. During half time at one of the games, I was in the girl's bathroom with all the varsity cheerleaders. They started giggling and sneaking a cigarette among themselves. They said that if I promised not to tell, they would give me an autographed picture of somebody named Elvis. I never told and they never gave me a picture of Elvis either!

As Mary and I settled into our new family, our ties became even stronger. We knew the safety and security of belonging— and the fun. For instance, Daddy and Lamar arranged one of our favorite family games while Mama, Mary, and I went to town. When we came home, we would find a note on the kitchen table from Daddy. It would simply state, "Look in the oven." In the oven would be another note, "Look in the refrigerator." In the refrigerator, the note might read, "Look under Shirley's pillow" . . . and on . . . and on until we would finally find a note that would read: "Gone to the school—will be home in an hour. Love, Daddy and Lamar!" What fun to belong!

It was at the big house in Butler that Mary and I finally broached a philosophical and spiritual discussion about God. One of us always asked the blessing before eating any family meal. That is, unless we had very important company, and then Daddy would pray a special prayer.

Mary and I discussed for days why we always said, "Ah men" instead of "Ah women" or something else. One night, when the chairman of the school board was having dinner with us, Daddy decided that we were ready to pray publicly. He asked Mary to say the blessing. Just before she began, she glanced at me. The glint in her eye forewarned me! I feared what was coming. My heart began to beat faster and faster as she hurried through the prayer. At the end of the blessing, Mary finished with *Ah Daddy*.

I held my breath! Mama was mortified, and exclaimed, "Mary Ellen!" Lamar stifled a laugh. Daddy grinned.

"Well, we always say *Ah men*," Mary very reasonably replied, "and Daddy *is* a man." I figured that, if they kept us after that episode, we were home for good! They did and we were!

The big house in Butler was grand. The tin roof sang during the spring rains. The porch was large enough to hold several rockers for adults to watch children at play. The high ceilings, coupled with open windows and fans, kept us cool on the hottest of summer days. The cellar gave just enough hints of darkness and mystery to keep our imaginations satisfied.

The house was also a safe house, filled with love and laughter, and it served an important purpose in my childhood. It provided large enough boundaries to let us discover a much bigger and safer world than we had ever known.

It was in the big house in Butler that two very special relationships developed. I understood clearly for the first time what a mama was supposed to do. She found the diamond in the rough. She knew I had potential, she knew I needed encouragement, and most of all, she knew I just needed some very special time with a Mama.

The second relationship—an understanding of letters, words, reading, and books also took place in that big house. I developed a lifelong love for reading and writing.

I've always felt that my passion for looking for the diamond in the rough and my passion for teaching and sharing stemmed from the big house in Butler. It is just the natural progression of things, the order of life and learning.

Aunt Audie—Bigger Than Life!

"She must weigh a thousand pounds!"

At least that is what my cousins and I would whisper when we got together. After all, Aunt Audie was the heaviest person we knew. But on that rich, love-filled body was the most comfortable lap in the world!

And how we loved her lap. It was so soft that we could snuggle our entire bodies into a magical place of comfort—accentuated with the pungent aromas of talcum powder, Lifebuoy soap, and Dove soap (one for her body, one for her face).

Yet Aunt Audie's massive form offered more than a lap. The skin on the bottom of her arms was like huge, pliable mounds of dough. She never seemed to notice my fascination with their softness or the way I would gently push into the flesh, just to see how far my hand could bury into her body.

During the school year, she was Miss Audie, the most sought-after first-grade teacher at the school Mary and I attended. And with good reason. As one of her former students recently told me, "Being hugged by Miss Audie was like being hugged by two pillows!" First graders love being hugged by two pillows!

However, in the summertime, she was simply Aunt Audie, and she belonged to Mary and me.

Aunt Audie was Daddy's twin sister and the kind of aunt every kid loved to visit. She lived on the family homestead in Bowdon Junction, Georgia, and she still slept in the very room where she and Daddy were born. The property was filled with old barns, outbuildings, a smokehouse, a tornado cellar, and fruit trees and bushes of every kind. It was a paradise for children—that is, after they finished their chores. Aunt Audie's obsession with cleanliness was dismaying to her visiting nieces and nephews. And the most dreaded chore that she assigned was to dust her salt-and-pepper-shaker collection.

You see, Aunt Audie had the biggest salt-and-pepper-shaker collection in the whole world. It filled three curio cabinets and several knick-knack shelves on the walls of the living room. Every salt shaker had a matching pepper shaker—every set perfect and complete. No broken or mismatched pieces in Aunt Audie's collection!

My favorite set was the miniature beer steins from Germany. It was a little embarrassing to love these so much—especially since I knew that we Southern Baptists did not approve of alcohol. At church, we even had grape juice for the Lord's Supper. I tried to appear casual as I located those shakers on one of the higher shelves. I glanced around to calculate whether or not anyone could actually read my mind as I picked them up.

In my imagination, I traveled halfway around the world. I pictured the people who might sit around drinking beer out of such glorious mugs—soldiers with young girls dreaming of possibilities and old men leaning on their elbows, swirling the contents of their mugs while dreaming of lost opportunities. I pictured robust, swaggering men telling lewd jokes, slapping a female's ample rump. Where in the world did those images come from? I guess this nine-year-old girl's knowledge of taverns, barrooms, and robust, swaggering men was limited to television's *Zorro*, *Bonanza*, and *Gunsmoke*.

I relished the idea that there was a world outside the very naive existence I was experiencing. And the fact that someone (probably an uncle stationed in Germany) sent a token of that world into our stable, wholesome, Southern world fascinated me. I was even more intrigued that the beer stein replicas remained in full view of anyone enthralled with the salt and pepper collection—the preacher, a deacon from the church, small children, and an imaginative girl.

The travels of all of the family members were chronicled on Aunt Audie's shelves. There were flamingo shakers from Florida, bears from the Great Smokey Mountains, and Aunt Jemimas from Mississippi. There were even Geisha girls *made in Taiwan*. Those salt-and-pepper shakers stood like picture postcard greetings from Washington, Canada, New Orleans, Texas, the Empire State Building, and Niagara Falls. Aunt Audie's collection from souvenir shops around the world enhanced my earliest lessons of life beyond school and church.

I loved the drifting thoughts that the souvenirs conjured up, but truthfully, my relationship with the salt and pepper shakers vacillated between love and hate. I hated having to dust her collection. So many pieces. So little. So fragile.

I hated the cats that collected dust in their curved tails, the intricate details on the gingerbread houses, and the minuscule spaces between each salt and pepper shaker on the shelf. The only way I was sure that I was going to get a nod of approval from Aunt Audie—and permission to go back outside and play—was to remove the entire collection, dust the shelf, and then replace each piece one by one. Of course, the job might not have taken so much time if I had not gotten lost in the dreams of lands and people that seemed planets away from the lazy days of summertime at Aunt Audie's.

She was single (it was whispered that she was an *old maid*) and Aunt Audie was set in her ways. In addition to cleanliness, she was passionate about cooking. Aunt Audie didn't get the size she was without having an intimate relationship with food. And, as you might have guessed, Aunt Audie could cook, and cook, and cook. She did everything in a big way.

Every single day, she made homemade biscuits. Memories of those warm, butter-melting biscuits still make my stomach growl and my taste buds respond like Pavlov's dogs. I have a distinct image of Aunt Audie pouring milk into a mound of flour in a large, heavy, wooden bread bowl, then squeezing lard into the mixture for the perfect texture—that delicate balance that kept biscuits from being either too heavy or too dry.

I can see her plump, flour-covered hands patting the biscuits into perfect doughy circles before placing them into the grease-coated, blackened biscuit pans. And then sliding the pans into the oven where they baked while she stirred gravy. I can still hear, see, and smell the flour sizzling into hot sausage grease, turning just the right shade of brown. And then she added milk, creating an ocean of rich gravy with bits of browned sausage floating around like buoys. Now that's the kind of gravy that made Aunt Audie FAT!

I remember one morning when Aunt Audie fixed fried chicken and gravy for breakfast—just because she knew it was my favorite! And years later, I watched and worked with her as she taught me how to create the perfect country-fried steak that was sometimes part of our noon meal. She was rather bossy when she was teaching me to cook, but if I paid attention, I learned.

Aunt Audie loved teaching more than anything—even more than making biscuits. Teaching school and training children was Aunt Audie's life. The first-graders in Miss Audie's classroom received much more than an educational foundation. They got to make plaster of Paris statues for every occasion. A child didn't move on to second grade without making pilgrims, snowmen, Santas, angels, bunnies, and other holiday and religious icons in plaster of Paris.

Her red rubber molds were as much a part of the first grade experience as the perfected curves of the ABCs. When the plaster of Paris was mixed (it had a mild chalky taste, I recall) and poured into the molds, time seemed to stand still. It seemed to be forever until the next day and Miss Audie's nod and declaration, "Yes, they're ready."

Watching Aunt Audie soap up her hands to remove the rubber mold was no less important than waiting for a great art teacher to unveil a masterpiece. As ducks, clowns, and turkeys began to appear in their white splendor, the proud creators would hold their breaths until it was clear that all the ears were in place, legs had not broken off, and air holes were nonexistent.

Then the art would begin. Painting with the passion of Van Gogh and the imagination of Picasso, every child knew their mama was going to be surprised and delighted by the holiday gift. Many homes in Carroll County, Georgia, were decorated for the holidays by the crafts of Miss Audie's children.

Though the figures probably failed to last more than a few years, the lesson endured a lifetime. Children who learned to read, to sing, to play in the marching band, to pray, to pledge allegiance, to make objects of Great Art, and to say "ma'am" continue to share their enthusiasm for discovery because they were blessed with being in Miss Audie's first grade.

When summer came and school was over for the year, it was our turn to have most of Aunt Audie's attention. Spending summer time with her was splendid! I got to attend an extra vacation Bible school, learn all the words to *How Great Thou Art* at summer revival, watch *As The World Turns* every afternoon, and sleep on a very old, carved bed at night. Unless I was scared. Then I slept on the day bed in Aunt Audie's room.

Sometimes we cried through *Queen for a Day*, or I helped Aunt Audie wash clothes outside on the back porch using an old wringer machine. We usually walked across the road to Larkin's house at least once during the summer. He was a lifelong neighbor of Aunt Audie's and the community barber. Because he always cut Aunt Audie's hair, Mary and I let him cut ours too. It was kind of weird having a man cut our hair, but some things we did just because Aunt Audie thought they needed to be done. Mama wasn't always happy with those haircuts. (Looking back at school pictures taken in the early fall, I can see Mama's concern!)

During the summer, I was allowed to explore the second floor of the house. Upstairs there was one very large bedroom filled with double beds and trunks. And tucked away off the end of the bedroom was a special hideaway room. The ceiling sloped halfway down to where the wall and the dirty window overlooked the front yard of the house. Hundreds of very old, dusty books lined the walls of that room. They had belonged to my grandfather and were mostly about religion and education.

The stairs leading up to the second floor of the house were rather steep so Aunt Audie didn't go up there to clean much. I used this private place and time to sneak-a-peek at *True Romance*, Aunt Audie's favorite magazine. *True Romance* gave me my first insight into the desires of a woman's heart, the pain of failed relationships, and the ecstasy of love. I don't think Mama wanted me to read those stories, but I just couldn't help myself!

One summer, Aunt Audie and I watched a young, handsome John Kennedy accept his nomination for the presidency. Even though he was a Catholic, we decided that we were going to vote for him. As Aunt Audie said, "You don't have to tell anyone how you cast your vote for President."

A couple of years later, in the fall, I watched Aunt Audie tearfully mourn the death of the good-looking President Kennedy. I wasn't sure why we were so sad, but Aunt Audie explained that our world would probably never be the same. Then she put on her funeral dress for the day and wore it out of respect.

Dresses were as much a part of Aunt Audie as biscuits and plaster of Paris. During summer vacation, Aunt Audie worked on her wardrobe. All her dresses were cut from the exact same pattern—gathered skirt on a waistband, buttoned in front, collared, and later starched stiff. The color and design of the fabric changed to suit the occasion. Plaids, checks, and stripes for teaching school, dressy prints and florals for church, dark somber colors for funerals, and washed out cottons for around the house. Every year, Aunt Audie would make a very special dress for Easter, one that she wore with a matching hat, white gloves, patent leather shoes, and her summer Sunday pocketbook.

The textures of the dress material were just as varied as the prints: corduroys, denim, and wool for winter; heavy cotton and twill for the fall; and seersucker and polished cotton for spring and summer. Today, when I reach for an old family quilt, I'm often startled to see a piece of Aunt Audie's wardrobe stitched into the pattern, and I know just when and where she would have worn the dress.

Oh, how I remember those dresses and the starch. Aunt Audie had a passion for starch. Her dresses were as stiff as cardboard paper dolls as they hung on the clothesline held by wooden clothespins. If a dress had fallen off the line, it would have stood at attention on the ground. She could have been the poster child for Argo starch!

Aunt Audie starched everything, not just her dresses. She starched her cotton slips and *bras*—great big bras that blew in the summer breezes. While I loved the feel and smell of those line-dried clothes, I loved to peek at those *magnificent* bras! When they were fastened to the clothesline, they hung as close to the ground as her dresses. I couldn't help but be amazed at the size of the cups and the length of the bras. When would I ever grow up?

Mary and I thought we were Aunt Audie's favorites. After all, she was *our* Daddy's twin—something none of the other cousins could claim. As infants, she and Daddy were referred to as Boy and Girl, pet names that lived on for generations at family reunions. Looking at the baby picture of the two smiling, cherubic infants, our own kinfolk still end up in heated discussion about which one is Boy and which is Girl. The lacy baby dresses don't give away the secret.

According to family history, when they were children Aunt Audie petted and looked after Daddy—she even carried his books to school for him. When they became adults, Daddy gave much of his time and patience to looking after Aunt Audie.

I realize now that, through the years, all of her nieces and nephews held a special place in Aunt Audie's heart—and all of them have their own Aunt Audie story!

It's been almost thirty years since Aunt Audie's large, beautiful body wore out. The funeral was held at the church next door to the family homeplace. Not wanting to miss too much of my sophomore college days, I zipped home from school just in time to join my family as we walked into the church to pay a final tribute. At the time, I did not realize that a big part of who I am would always be connected with who Aunt Audie was. I thought I was saying good-bye to an aunt. Now I know that I was saying good-bye to a teacher, a mentor, and an imagination maker.

Just a few years ago, Boy joined Girl for their final reunion. I like to believe that as they met in Heaven, Daddy and Aunt Audie (starched wings and all) made the perfect, flawless, unbroken set—much like those wonderful salt and pepper shakers that were such a part of Aunt Audie's life, and mine too.

Not-So-Vacant Lot

There are individual "best friends" and then there are families who are "best friends." Our family best friends were the Williamsons. Mr. Williamson was a high school science teacher, a photographer with a mysterious dark room, and a tinker of all kinds of gadgets and machines. Miss Inez, his wife, was a fourth-grade teacher, a homemaker, and a full-time mom to their three sons—Greg, Mike, and Teddy (whom we called "the boys"). Mike and I were the same age, as were Mary and Teddy. Greg was the oldest of us all (except for Lamar, who was too old to play with us). That made Greg the boss.

Our families were so close that, when Daddy got a new job as a principal, Mr. Williamson agreed to relocate to be his science teacher. In the late 1950s, we all moved to Villa Rica, Georgia, where we rented houses on the same street.

Our neighborhood was located behind a hosiery mill. The water runoff from the mill formed a ditch next door to the Williamsons. We loved to stand at the edge of the ditch and watch the dyes rush into the sewage pipe that went under the road, down the ditch, and out of sight. The dye was hot and foamy and multicolored, depending on the color of the socks. That ditch, too, was the subject of a lot of speculation on our part. We wondered what it would be like to get in a boat and follow the stream to the end. We'd drop plastic toys and watch them drift out of our lives to who knew where—probably the Atlantic Ocean. I'm sure the EPA has now done away with hot, foamy dye ditches and the fascination that goes along with them. At least I hope so.

One hot, summer day, we were busy jumping the ditch and waiting for Daddy and Mr. Williamson to get home from south Georgia with a truckload of fresh peaches. They got back late in the afternoon and the peeling and canning and freezing began. Days passed before the last of the peaches were freed of pits and put away for winter pleasures.

The best part of a truckload of peaches was having enough left over to make homemade peach ice cream. Late evenings, after supper and before the sun went down, we all stopped our peach-work long enough to make a churn of ice cream. It was an exciting ordeal—even a lot more exciting than going to the Dairy Queen or drugstore. I would dance around impatiently, watching the rock salt create a crusty film on the wooden ice cream bucket. All the kids stopped chasing lightning bugs long enough to beg for a chance to turn the crank. I never really understood how Miss Inez knew when the ice cream was ready, but she did. She would suddenly appear with Dixie cups and spoons, remove the dasher, and dish out the world's best ice cream. Somehow, during those summer nights, I knew that God was in Heaven and all was right in our world. Best friends make the best ice cream, I believe.

When our two families began to plan for permanent homes (instead of rentals), both families decided to build across the street from the new high school. That was the first house Daddy and Mama had ever built and we all were excited. Lamar headed off to college, but he still got his own room. Mary and I shared a new room and even got to pick out the paint color for the walls.

The Williamson family built their house very close to ours (only one vacant lot separating the yards) so we could all play together. This lot became known as Center Lot, and for a while it became the center of my childhood world.

We had to get permission to go to the Williamsons' house, but not to go to Center Lot. Before the two houses were completed, there was already a wide path in the middle of the broom sage, leading from one home to the other. Pretty soon we had trampled and played in Center Lot enough to rid it of almost all the standing broom sage.

Center Lot could have also been called Center Stage. It was the arena where five preadolescent kids created life adventures. Once, we used rocks to form the outline of a western town, kind of like the one in *Gunsmoke*. It was a big town with a wide road down the middle—a jail, bank, and saloon lined one side of the road, houses and other buildings lined the other side. Of course, I imagined myself as Miss Kitty, the owner of the saloon, although I knew we were not supposed to drink alcohol. I loved to serve a shot of whiskey to Mike or Greg, who took turns being the town sheriff or any one of a number of heroes. The youngest two, Mary and Teddy, were stuck with being the bank robbers, outlaws, *Injuns,* and whoever else might end up in jail.

As we grew older and the boys developed a greater interest in sports, Center Lot became a baseball field. We never had enough players for two teams, so we played a lot of games with an imaginary man on base. Sometimes we played with all four bases, but more often than not, we only had one base—second base, directly behind the pitcher. Greg, being the boss, was usually the pitcher. Mary and I got stuck with being the catchers and chasing their foul balls and wild pitches to the ditch by the road.

Life was carefree and fun for us kids, but probably a little more stressful for the grown-ups. Daddy's doctor told him he needed to relax more, so he took up golf. Oh, how his men friends laughed about Daddy chasing a little white ball around a pasture. It wasn't long, though, before the neighborhood men and uncles were leaving home on Saturday morning for a round of golf. And it wasn't too long before we turned Center Lot into our own golf course. We buried cans and had golf tournaments like those in Augusta, 200 miles away. The Williamsons even planted the requisite azaleas!

At one point, the boys got a motorized go-cart. This led to what might have been the most exciting of Center Lot's transformations. Suddenly it was a go-cart course, complete with a large outer circle and a figure-eight inner circle. Part of the track was left over from baseball and bike trails—we just had to remove the bicycle jump that had been built for our cycling days.

When the go-cart was working, we would ride round and round and round. Of course, because it was a dangerous toy, Mary and I couldn't ride without permission. The go-cart belonged to the boys and they were always tinkering with screwdrivers and pliers and other such tools to get it to run. I was mesmerized that they could figure out just which wire to bend or screw to turn, and, voile!, we could ride again. Looking back, I realize they inherited their Dad's tinkering traits.

One day, our life on Center Lot was threatened. A nice car parked on the road beside Center Lot and an older man and woman got out, along with a well-dressed younger man. Knowing this might mean trouble, I immediately ran to find Mama. She would figure out what was going on. She told me that she thought the strangers wanted to buy the lot and build a house on it. I couldn't believe it could happen. Wasn't Center Lot *ours*?

Mama conferred with Daddy then they quickly called the Williamsons. Discreetly, we were encouraged by our parents to go outside and act like kids—*really* act like kids, while the three strangers walked through Center Lot. We needed no encouragement. We hooped and hollered and yelled and shouted from yard to yard. We rode our bicycles, performing daredevil stunts. The boys got the go-cart running and we took turn zooming around our speedway. We laughed and screeched about the snake we found crawling across the baseball diamond one day. The car drove away. The next day, Mr. Williamson and Daddy bought the lot.

Of course, our lives weren't limited to Center Lot. Mama and Daddy and the Williamsons loved to play cards—mostly Rook and Canasta. They played for hours on end while the five children played games too. At the boys' house, we played with army men and model planes. At our house, we played with puzzles and board games, for we never did get the boys to play house with our dolls.

I never knew who had more fun: the kids or the grown-ups. There were always lots of laughs and giggles at the card table as one couple would barely beat the other. Many nights the kids were awakened in the middle of the night to trek home after our parents had had their fill of cards, fun, and dessert at their best friends' house. It was a glorious time.

We were two families, complete with children who loved each other and parents who had lots of dreams and aspirations for their children. Our lives intertwined through school politics, church, holidays, and meals. When Miss Inez made Christmas stockings for her boys, she made matching ones for Mary and me. We went with the Williamsons to visit their Granddaddy's farm in the country, where we sat around and carved wooden whistles from Poplar tree branches. We were more than just two families. We were Best Friends Families.

In 1963, our family moved away. This time the Williamson family stayed behind. Mr. Williamson became the high school principal, and when we were in our teens, Miss Inez surprised us all by having a baby girl. Mary and I always believed that Miss Inez missed us so much that she decided to have her own daughter.

One day we got a phone call from Miss Inez. Her son, my friend, the child-sheriff and favorite go-cart driver, Mike, had a tumor at the base of his brain. It would have to be operated on. I still get a lump in my throat when I think of Mike with his pretty blue eyes and long eyelashes undergoing such a dangerous operation. While the doctors were able to save his life, the carefree, spirited boy of my youth was gone. His growth and development would not progress normally. His life would become more challenging.

Not too long after Mike's surgery, Mr. Williamson died. Miss Inez was left to complete the raising of her family. Everybody else was simply left with broken hearts.

As fate would have it, Teddy married the girl next door— not Mary, but the sister in the family who bought our house after we moved away.

Just a few years ago, Mama, Miss Inez, and I went out to dinner together to celebrate Mama's 78th birthday. As we reminisced about the years of my childhood, I thanked her again for my stocking, which I have hung every Christmas for the past forty years.

When we arrived back at her house, Miss Inez invited me in and gave me a porcelain nativity scene (a crèche)—another treasured addition to my adult home.

Every time I unpack my old felt stocking and unwrap my nativity scene, my thoughts turn to all the dreams, hopes, and expectations of those two couples who raised their children together.

And, sometimes, on a warm summer night filled with lightning bugs, I can hear the sounds of cards shuffling, noises from Center Lot, and the grinding of the ice cream crank making the best homemade peach ice cream in the world. I am reminded that we all need two things in life: a Center Lot to safely explore all the crazy, wacky dimensions of self, and Best Friends to support us, love us, and help us grow up in a wonderful way.

A Horse of A Different Color

School stores, like recess, seem to be a thing of the past. But when I went to school, both were an integral part of the day. In fact, recess was for playing AND for going to the school store. There we could buy Cokes, snacks, ice cream, and school supplies like notebook paper and number two pencils.

The first school store I remember was a little brick addition to the high school, just down the sidewalk from the elementary school building. Inside there was a Coca-Cola machine that was operated by a crank and a caged area where the lucky high school kids got to be the storekeepers.

I couldn't wait for the recess bell to ring. I would walk as fast as my legs could carry me, down the oil-slicked wooden hallway floors, out the door, down the steps (two at a time), to the school store. More often than not, I would get there only to discover that I had left my money in my desk. Not to worry. Thad, the school custodian, was always just outside the school store rolling a cigarette with Prince Albert tobacco. He seemed to know when I was short a nickel or two. I'm not sure that I really ever thanked him, but I do know that the nickel allowed me to buy the Tom's Peanuts that I needed to make my Coke perfect.

Daddy had taught me how to open just one corner of the peanut bag (I usually used my teeth, even though I wasn't supposed to), create a funnel around the Coke bottle with my hand, and pour an entire pouch of peanuts into a Coca-Cola for a scrumptious treat. I had to drink a couple of sips first, though, or the liquid would spill over. I loved those peanut Cokes, and I loved Thad for making sure I had one almost every day.

The biggest commodities at the school store other than Cokes was notebook paper and lined writing tablets. Blue Horse was the only brand of school paper sold. Each package or notebook came with a coupon valued from 5 to 25 points. Kids knew we could collect the little square coupons and mail them in for wonderful prizes; at least that's what was promised in print on the inside of the wrapper that went around the paper packages and notebooks.

A zillion Blue Horses was all it took to get a bicycle—and I was determined to get one. Actually, I think it was just a few thousand, but when I first started collecting Blue Horses, it seemed like a zillion.

I studied the flyer that described the prizes and decided that, yes, I too could be the proud owner of a bright and shiny Blue Horse bicycle. All I would have to do is save—and save I did. Now, there was no way I was ever going to buy enough paper and notebooks to earn the points on my own, so I devised a method of getting the most points I could. It was a simple plan. I was good at creating plans.

Since Daddy was the school principal and Mama was a teacher, Mary and I had to hang around the school in the afternoons for them to finish up their day. I figured that if I could beat Thad to the trash collection, I could go through the waste cans and find the thrown-away Blue Horse coupons. It wasn't long before my enterprising behavior got noticed. Teachers began to save Blue Horses and Thad kept any he found just for me. Mama asked her students to save theirs, and Daddy's secretary kept an eye out for any in the office. It seemed like the whole school was saving Blue Horses. For me!

At the time, I thought I was doing 90% of the saving, with just a little bit of help along the way. In retrospect, I probably only saved 10% of the Blue Horses. But, remember, I was the one with the plan!

Finally, the day of counting and ordering arrived. I cut and stacked coupons of the same value. Then I added, tallied, and totaled. I checked my count two, then three times. Not only did I have enough Blue Horses for a bicycle, I had some to spare! It was exciting to calculate how to best spend the excess. I spent hours pouring over the catalogue to find just the right prizes. I wanted to use every single one of my Blue Horse coupons.

Finally, after much deliberation, I discovered that there were two other prizes I could not live without: a chemistry set (complete with chemicals in vials and flasks and shakers for mixing) and a Jon Nagy Learn-To-Draw Kit. My heart was thudding as I tallied the final count. Yes, I could have it all: a bicycle, a chemistry set, and an art set! Life was good to this fifth grader.

It seemed like it took forever before the prizes came. Some skeptics didn't believe Blue Horse was really going to send them. I never lost hope. Every day I would rush home from school to see if my packages had arrived. I worried about the postal system and dreamed of Blue Horse thieves. Finally, one spring afternoon, the long-anticipated prizes were delivered.

It was a beautiful bike, a real girl's bike—the kind that

didn't have a center bar. Blue, with a white stripe, silver handle
bars without a trace of rust, white stripes on the tires, and a
wonderful black seat. I learned all sorts of incredible tricks on
that bike. I could ride with both my hands thrust to the sky. I
could ride with my feet across the handlebars and my hands
crossed behind my head, as if I were lying on a couch. When
Mama wasn't looking, I would put my feet on the seat and
straighten my legs, still holding onto the handles. I looked like
an inverted-V as I guided that bicycle down the hill. (I never did
just stand up on the seat with no hands—even I had my limits.)

Mary and I loved to ride together. Sometimes the extra
person rode on the handlebars, sometimes on the back fender.
After a while, we realized the fender wouldn't last long if we kept
riding on it, so we learned to ride with one of us pedaling (in a
standing position) and the other sitting on the seat. It was
wonderful! It was magnificent! It was freedom! It was LIFE!

The chemistry set was great for indoor days. I spent hours
fascinated with the instructions. It kind of reminded me of
cooking. I just put ingredients together to make something else.
I was mesmerized by the names of things I couldn't pronounce.
I was serious about measuring and mixing and pouring—yet
afraid I might create an explosion that would get me in a lot of
trouble. Most of all, I loved how the two red metal doors of the
chemistry set opened to reveal bottles and vials and tubes and
stuff, all neatly organized in metal holders. I so wanted to keep
everything in order.

I also thought I would become a famous artist before the
school year was over. With my new art kit, it seemed that
drawing would be easy. After all, with the thick paper, chalk,
and gooey eraser, all I had to do was follow the instructions to
create puppy faces, kittens, flowers, and scenes like I saw from

the car window riding through the country. But, it seemed that the more I tried, the uglier my pictures became. I drew with my chalk, blended with a tissue, and rubbed with the eraser until I had a gray mass of NOTHING! It was discouraging and mysterious. How do artists really make a beautiful picture? I never did learn the answer to that question.

Blue Horses—what a memory! Every time one of my grandchildren wants to clip a coupon off a cereal box and save it to get a prize, I pull out the scissors, clip, and store the coupon. However, what is considered a prize this month is old news and boring by next month. The prizes change almost as quickly as the boxes are emptied, at least much too fast for the occasional weekends at our house. Today's cereal boxes advertise a product like "Smud" (Silly Putty) or a digital watch or backpack. I know these are wonderful prizes, but not one is a bicycle, a chemistry set, or a Jon Nagy Learn-To-Draw Kit.

Every year or so, I clean out the drawer and throw the coupons away. We've yet to be consistent enough to save the right quantity of bar codes from the boxes to get the prize they want. Besides, we don't have a whole school helping us and bar codes are not nearly as appealing as Blue Horses.

My blue bicycle lasted a long time and gave me many miles of adventures and daredevil stunts. The chemistry set was eventually tossed—empty chemical jars, blue granules, and rust marring the once-meticulous inside. Jon Nagy was given away—hopefully to a budding artist. I don't remember who.

I still have a bicycle. It belonged to my husband's youngest son, Matt. When he graduated from high school and needed a newer, more sophisticated and sportier bike for college, he left the old one behind. It's not really pretty. It's mostly black with a little bit of green. It doesn't have a back fender and the handlebars turn down instead of up. Truthfully, the seat was a little small for me, so I replaced it with an extra-wide one. I never have figured out how to use all the gears, but I still ride without my hands (when Randy is not looking).

Most of my mixing, measuring, and pouring takes place in the kitchen now, and I do have two watercolor sets that I dabble with occasionally. I am still curious about what makes things work and how artists are able to create masterpieces.

Blue Horses and Thad are long gone, but both fill a very special spot in my memory bank. I think I'll have a bottled Coca-Cola with peanuts in it and toast them both!

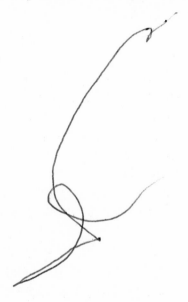

Wanted:

Life Outside this Small Town

I love going to the post office. I go almost every day and enjoy seeing the townspeople. I pass time with the ones I know, and nod to the ones I don't know. I love the energy of people sending letters or big stacks of invitations or holiday cards. Standing in line waiting for people to pick up packages or buy stamps, my mind often drifts back to the Cassville Post Office.

Just before my thirteenth birthday, our family moved from the small Georgia town of Villa Rica to an even smaller community of about 300 people. Daddy was the principal of the county high school and Mama was the guidance counselor. The school system furnished us with a *teacherage*. A teacherage is to a principal what a parsonage is to a preacher: a place to live. Our house was on the school campus and we ended up living there for ten years. From my bedroom window, I could see the school complex. The Baptist church was directly across the front yard, and about a half-mile down the road was the community of Cassville, Georgia.

Cassville consisted of a general store and what people

jokingly referred to as a lean-to post office. Actually, the post office was a structurally sound building that dated to pre-Civil War days, and for a while it became the center of my world.

We didn't have mail delivery in Cassville, so each day (except Sundays), I walked or rode my bike to the post office. We didn't have a post office box, so our mailing address was "General Delivery, Cassville, Georgia," which simply meant that Miss Reba handed us our mail through the window box inside the post office. Miss Reba was the real reason I wanted to go to the post office.

Miss Reba was the keeper of all that happened back behind the window—a mysterious place of stamps, scales, packages, and stacks of mail. Those visits to the post office and Miss Reba were an open window to the world for me.

The public area of the post office was about four feet by ten feet. A door, with a window on each side, made up the front of the building. Once inside, you were directly in front of Miss Reba's window. To the left of the door a bench for sitting and visiting. On the wall to the left of the bench was a bulletin board where the current MOST WANTED flyers were posted.

I was fascinated with the pictures of men who would do something so bad or dangerous that their very unflattering photograph would be displayed on the wall in Cassville, Georgia, for all our world to see. I feigned an interest in something else on the board as I studied the crimes—*forgery, fugitive,* and *embezzlement* were foreign words to me, but I knew what *murder, kidnapping,* and *rape* meant (at least I thought I did). I would memorize the faces for both my personal protection and the opportunity to help the FBI catch a criminal.

My imagination drifted to scenes vacillating between fright and heroism. I envisioned one of those fugitives stopping me on my bike and asking for directions to get out of town. I imagined that I wouldn't get close enough to their car for them to nab me for a kidnap ransom, but I would get just close enough to let them think I was a helping neighbor.

I had it all figured out. I would give false directions, sending them to the local Confederate cemetery. This would force them to make several confusing turns and delay their escape. Then I would furiously pedal to the Kennedys', the Tribbles', the parsonage, or the post office (whichever was closest) and call the Sheriff. I was ready for a reward, a Medal of Honor, and most of all, the triumphant accolades that would come because I had made our world a safer place.

Needless to say, the only people who stopped and asked directions in Cassville were families who had detoured from Highway 41 (the major route between the northern states and Florida) and were looking for a place to eat. You see, if you were a visitor in Cassville and a local family didn't invite you to dinner or you didn't eat at a church, you had to go eleven miles to the nearest restaurant.

The MOST WANTED posters took up precious little of my time at the post office. But I must admit, the first time I noticed a woman on a wanted poster, I fantasized for hours about what kind of life adventures she must have experienced to become a criminal. A woman crook. That was beyond the scope of even my imagination.

As I said, my main reason for going to the Cassville Post Office was to talk with Miss Reba. Although she was married and had a grown son, she was always *Miss* Reba to me. Wearing her lightly starched blouses with laced trim collars, she stood at the window for an hour at a time as we discussed Sunday's sermon, the church choir, the new neighbors, or world events.

World events were intruding on our idyllic small-town life in ways unheard of in its hundred-year history. The same day I started high school, black students began to attend our school. Integration was total for our county, meaning that black and white kids attended school together at the formerly segregated schools. It was a very big deal, especially in rural Georgia.

Miss Reba and I discussed at length the rightness of the situation. I had no clues about the really volatile issues—only that it seemed to me to be the right thing to do. Miss Reba anxiously awaited my visit after the first day of school to hear what happened.

After school, I changed out of my new dress and into my shorts and Keds, jumped onto my bike, and pedaled as fast as I could to the post office.

"It was a good day, nothing really happened." I said. "Daddy welcomed us and kinda made a challenge for a great school year. Mama says he does that every year." I reported. "He did say he wanted to especially welcome all the new students, and then he started clapping his hands until everybody was clapping. It was just like we were cheering for our football team. Some people are already saying how much better our team is going to be now that we have some black boys to play." None of us knew then that such remarks could be considered offensive.

I was much more excited to talk about being in high school with all the new kids from other county elementary schools than discussing how many blacks were in my classes and whether or not I had a black teacher. Miss Reba picked right up on that and we changed the subject . . . something we did a lot.

The greatest thing about the post office was that it was the local stop for the bookmobile—an incredible vehicle that brought the outside world into Cassville. Every other Thursday, enough books were left at the post office to fill the two shelves behind the door. (Later I learned that the very first bookmobile ever started in my current hometown of Carrollton, Georgia, making books possible for other rural counties and communities.)

Miss Reba and I loved to read. We shared the same taste in books—romantic, historical novels. We devoured *Plantation Trilogy*, lamenting the bygone lifestyle of plantation days and hoop skirts. We tended to avoid discussing the realities or morality of slavery. I finally got all the way through *Gone With the Wind* and romanticized about Rhett Butler for weeks. Our books created a magical world for both of us.

I could barely contain myself with excitement on the every-other-Thursday that the bookmobile stopped at the post office. I couldn't wait to see the new books. I minded my manners and said the perfunctory hello to Miss Reba before quickly closing the post office door. Right there, on two shelves spanning the wall behind the door, were the new books—each one a treasure chest waiting to be opened.

I would stretch on tiptoes to read the titles on the top row, quickly glancing over each title and then coming back to savor the ones that seemed the most exciting. I loved the books with clear plastic covers over bright, enticing book jackets. Miss Reba reminded me not to "judge a book by its cover," but I just couldn't help it. I imagined that books with emotionally stirring covers would contain stories that would teach me the mysteries of love and romance. Or, if I were lucky, maybe I'd learn a little about sex (even though I *never* discussed interest in the latter). I wasn't sure Miss Reba knew about these things, and even if she did, I somehow had the idea that it was not a subject for our discussions.

Although I didn't have the vocabulary to describe it then, what I know now was that Miss Reba was a romanticist. We talked of relationships, romances, and far-away places. When we were talking together I think other residents felt like intruders when they entered the post office for their mail. It wasn't that we were rude ... in fact, we were always eager for any fresh gossip. But, somehow, other patrons sensed that they were only visitors in Miss Reba's and my special world. They were right.

Most of all, Miss Reba and I talked about books and far-away places. Miss Reba loved distant places, almost as much as she loved people. She traveled via *National Geographic* and the picture postcards sent to locals by vacationing friends and family. We discussed places we would go if we got a chance: Yellowstone . . . Mt. Rushmore . . . the Holy Land . . . Niagara Falls . . . the White House . . . Egypt . . . and on, and on.

And then I left the community of my youth. After high school I went away to college, returning to Cassville only during vacations to brag about what the real world was like. But I knew that Cassville Post Office represented a phase of my life that I was ready to leave behind. I wanted to be something else, something other than a rural girl with rural ways. In an attempt to poke fun at my hometown, my college friends would write me when I was home and address the letter: *Shirley, Cassville, Georgia.* Even though I encouraged them to address the letters that way, I knew what we were really doing was ridiculing the simple post office and our small community ways. I always got the letter—and always from Miss Reba.

Eventually, I did travel to Yellowstone, Mt. Rushmore, Niagara Falls, and the White House. And I feel a little shame when I try to remember whether or not I sent Miss Reba any postcards. I know I meant to, and I know she would have treasured them.

Now my life is one that I only dreamed about in my teens.

It is filled with travel and adventure. But when I need to regroup, I always find myself at a bookshelf looking over the latest selection of novels. After choosing a book (sometimes by its cover), I settle down to read and wonder what Miss Reba would have to say about the book.

I have a few special treasures from my days at the Cassville Post Office. On the table beside my reading chair, I have a photograph of the post office—a surprise gift one Christmas from my sister, Mary. Mary lives in Chattanooga, Tennessee, north of Cassville, Georgia. A couple of years ago, she took her new husband, Ruben, to visit the community of our high school years. While there, Mary visited with Miss Reba and together they made the treasure possible.

And amid my very special keepsakes is a beautiful depression-glass cake plate. Miss Reba sent it to me as a wedding gift. She had received the plate as a wedding gift for her own marriage forty years before. Every time I use the pink plate to serve cake or cookies to special guests, I am reminded of a simpler time in life—a time when the whole world lay open before me.

When I think of that naïve country girl with her dreams of adventure and romance, I realize that the real treasure in my life was not found in the adventures, or the travels, or the books. Rather, it was in the relationship between an extraordinarily gifted and intellectually curious Miss Reba and an eager, romantic, and starry-eyed schoolgirl.

Sew What!

O ne day, I was busy around the house when my neighbor, Margaret, called and asked if her great-granddaughter, Jessica, and her best friend, Ashley, could swim off our dock. Later, as I watched them laughing and horse playing, I recognized Mary and me at that same age. After dinner and another late-evening swim, Jessica and Ashley excitedly told me that they were going to learn to needlepoint before bedtime. Margaret was going to teach them how. I knew it didn't matter that almost 70 years separated Margaret and the girls. When they sat together—Jessica on one side of Margaret and Ashley on the other—they were just girls doing what girls love to do. Talking and laughing while passing down traditions.

During their time together, Margaret became their teacher, confidant, and girlfriend. When one became frustrated that the stitches were wrong, Margaret would patiently remind her that she must *undo* the stitch. "You just can't cover up a mistake," she often told them.

My mind immediately danced back in time to my own lessons in hand sewing and craft-making.

And the family stories that led to my lessons.

When Mama and Daddy first married, he said he figured out pretty quickly that Mama needed to go to college—she surely wasn't going to make it as a homemaker. The first of many jokes about Mama's cooking occurred when Grandmother Gillham left home to take Uncle Archie to Arizona for the asthma cure.

It was just a few weeks after my parents had married, and Granddaddy was supposed to eat lunch with the newlyweds every day while Grandmother was gone. He lasted only two days as a guest at Mama's table. He discovered that the biscuits were too hard to eat and sneaked them out to the hogs. He was dismayed to find them still in the trough two days later! Granddaddy started eating lunch at Smith's Café and Daddy joined him. That story has been retold a lot of times since 1940!

Because Daddy grew up in a home where all the girls were exceptionally skilled in homemaking (two of his sisters were home economists with the state), it took him a while to understand that all women are not created equal—at least with regard to homemaking skills. Thinking that, with the right incentive, Mama would manage the household chores common to girls of her generation, Daddy bought her a brand-new Singer sewing machine. He envisioned the curtains she would make for the rooms in the house where they boarded. Much to his chagrin, he arrived home early one afternoon to find Mama sitting at the machine, sobbing. Always the doting husband, he asked, "What's wrong, honey?" Between sobs she answered, "What in the world am I supposed to do with all this material?" After a full day she had yet to even thread the machine—she had not stitched one seam! Being a man of great compassion and extraordinarily good common sense, Daddy gave the sewing machine away. Probably to one of his sisters.

Mama had graduated with honors from high school, but didn't go to college immediately because her parents didn't believe that a girl needed a degree—just a husband. Besides, she wanted to be a nurse or a teacher and her parents didn't take to such fancy notions.

Daddy was more enlightened. As the local school principal, Daddy knew of three girls who needed a ride every day to the teachers' college in a neighboring town, so before she knew it, Mama was driving daddy's car, full of aspiring teachers. Each day she drove 60 miles round trip to attend college classes and discover her passion in life—teaching.

It's often said that parents want their children to learn the things they did not. So, at a very early age, Mary and I were taught to clean house, cook, and eventually delve into hand sewing. After all, all our grandmothers and aunts were craftswomen in one homemaking form or another.

When I was seven, I was given a weaving set to create potholders. How I loved the red metal frame with its four rows of spikes, standing straight as soldiers. My usually clumsy hands seemed to become graceful as I wove the hook in and out of the yarn. I pulled together colors that were beautiful beyond words. As I worked the edges to finish the potholder, I imagined myself sitting at ancient looms, weaving clothes for my family. The finished product was often a present for Mama or Aunt Audie or Miss Inez, or someone else who was deemed worthy of my talents. The neighborhood and family kitchens were filled with my crafts.

It didn't take too long before I outgrew potholders and began looking for other outlets for my budding talent as a seamstress. Grandmother Gillham, my Mama's mother, made quilts, but that task seemed too big, even for my enthusiasm. I bought colorful thread and tried my hand at appliqué and soft knitting yarns. But my embroidery threads always seemed to be in a knot and the knitting needles were too independent to conform to my style, so I quickly gave up.

Until I was 13.

When we moved to Cassville, Georgia, where the population of the *under 20 set* was limited to about 10, it didn't take me long to discover the magic of Miss Corrine. She lived on the other side of the Baptist Church. I figure she must have been about 80 when we moved in and was the kind of spinster who loved the attention of children, especially ones who were interested in all her *things*. Miss Corrine had needlepoint, crochet, knitting, tatting, embroidery, and pieced quilts on every surface of her home, including the beds and windows. Her dimly lit rooms were also filled with treasures from around the world. Miss Corrine's sister was a missionary in China and had sent a lot of fascinating gifts. I thought I might want to grow up to be a missionary to China, so that made visits to Miss Corrine's house even more special.

After a few visits, Miss Corrine decided to teach Mary and me to do some handcrafts. She seemed to have an innate understanding of my need to settle down and quietly work on a beautiful project. Handling the fabric and the needles somehow tamed my spirit and my whirling hormonal changes. The need for success was almost as strong as my need to create and my need for attention.

Miss Corrine decided that Mary and I would learn to Swedish weave and make fancy *finger towels*. Before we could touch the fabric, thread, or needle, we had to wash our hands, she said. Then we pulled a thread to determine the straight of the fabric and made a hem on each end. Like the potholders, the finished products became signature gifts for every adult who was my friend. I would secretly memorize the color scheme in a bathroom and then create towels that perfectly matched the decor. Of course, most bathrooms were pale green, yellow, or blue tile, so there wasn't a lot of room for imagination.

Miss Corrine also taught us how to count the stitches. The patterns went up like pyramids—across, up, and across some more, and down and out and down and out. Each pattern was repeated five to six times on the ends of the fingertip towel that would be folded and hung on a towel rack so guests could admire the stitching. There were moments of frustration when I discovered that the count was off or the pattern did not *come out* right on the sides. It was then I learned the lessons of patience and *undoing.*

How I loved those afternoons with Miss Corrine at my sewing lessons—choosing the color of the fabric and thread—choosing the design, trying to decide whether to make a simple pattern or a fancier, more complicated, intricate one.

In the winter, we sat in Miss Corrine's toasty sitting room in small chairs under bright lamps and worked quietly and quickly and with deep concentration on the project at hand. In the summer, we sat in the backyard beneath the shade trees and smelled the sweet aroma of gardenia and honeysuckle. My feet dangled off the lawn chair as I leaned over my lap to count and stitch. I believe it was in Miss Corrine's backyard that I discovered the joys of solitude.

Our conversations centered around church news, vacation Bible school, the upcoming homemade ice-cream social, the bumper-to-bumper traffic on highway 41 (those Yankees on their way to Florida), and the racial tension mounting in the deep South. We also discussed what was happening at school and the kids that came from all over the county to attend our school. And we learned bits and pieces of Miss Corrine's life and bits and pieces of Miss Corrine's wisdom.

After I had concentrated for a long time on the stitches, my legs would begin to twitch and my spirit would start to turn back into my tomboy self. About the same time, Miss Corrine would suggest that we stop and have a sugar-coated lemon drop—our favorite candy. After we ate the candy, we could not pick up our needles again because the sugar would turn the needles black. The lemon drops became the signal that the sewing lesson was over for the day.

In high school I took one year of home economics. I learned the basics of cooking, child-care, home care, and sewing. Daddy bought another sewing machine, this time for me, and I proudly made most of my own clothes. I selected fabrics fit for a queen and patterns that required a minimum number of buttonholes. I learned to set in sleeves, take in darts, baste, hem, *do* button-holes, create tucks, and finally *put in* zippers that were barely noticeable. I already knew how to *undo*—recognizing that no amount of pressing or snipping would cover up a crooked or puckered seam. I learned that from Miss Corrine.

When I got to college, I realized that other girls did not know how to make their own clothes, except for a roommate who was actually more of a clothes designer. It was obvious they didn't have a Miss Corrine as their friend. Actually, there was little time for the sewing machine unless a fraternity formal required a dress that I could ill afford off the racks at Parisian. But, eventually, I began to sew the skimpy halter-tops so necessary for my era. I don't think Miss Corrine would have been too thrilled about those.

Pretty soon the only finger work I did was embroidering blue jeans. My craft work consisted of decoupaging boxes for gifts for Mama and Daddy and weaving rings out of wire and beads. It was the '60s and early '70s and love beads were all the rage. They were a lot cheaper to make than to buy.

Somehow the sewing machine made its way from Cassville to Samford University, to Albuquerque, and back to Georgia. It sat for years in Uncle Leslie's basement until I needed a dress for the antebellum party Cousin Martha Jean and I were giving at our farmhouse. I also made a wedding gown for a student teacher who could not afford a store-bought dress. I remembered not wanting to spend so much money on a ready-made dress when I was in college. Eventually, the machine bobbin knotted one too many times, so I gave the machine away to the first person who showed any interest.

When my grandson, Zeke, was about seven years old, he was rambling through my sewing stool and announced that he wanted to hand sew. And sew we did. We cut a pattern for drawstring bags out of an old tablecloth. I taught him how to stitch the tops to make a pocket for the string, and then how to sew the sides together. He liked sewing. Zeke's only request was for "one of those silver things you put on your finger, Gran-Gran. The needle *hurts* when I push it through!"

When we finished, he had treasure bags for his mommy, other grandmothers, and a special bag for his cousin Nala's first birthday. For a while, whenever he tired of playing in the secret hut the boys had built or needed respite from the commotion of the day, he would suddenly announce, "Gran-Gran, I'm tired. I just want to sit down and sew."

As for my sewing, when Randy needs a pair of pants mended, he takes them next door to Margaret and she quickly and neatly makes them almost as good as new—well, certainly good enough for farm work. Given some extra time and a quiet moment, I will sew on a button or two. The real mending takes place next door, where a sewing machine stands ready at all times.

About eight years ago, when my friend, Linda, and I first came up with the idea of a neighborhood live nativity, I put myself in charge of the outfits. I sat busily and excitedly on the floor, measuring and cutting and basting and sewing seven angel skirts. Adorable little neighborhood girls wore the skirts with halos and wings as they danced, pranced, and finally kneeled around the Baby Jesus.

Each year, the skirts are passed down from sister to sister and neighbor to neighbor as roles and skirts are outgrown. New ones are made as the realm of angels grows. The Wise Men and shepherd costumes, quickly stitched out of pillowcases, dark wool, and remnants of gold and silver fabrics are stored away in my college trunk.

My thoughts about my own sewing escapades were abruptly interrupted when Margaret called. She talked about how Jessica and Ashley, two tomboys earlier in the evening, had settled into their sewing and their life lessons before going to bed. Before saying good night, they told Margaret that they would leave their teddy bear needlepoint with her—for another visit.

The next day, they returned to soccer, sports, and giggling phone calls . . . but I bet they took the needlepoint pattern books to dream up and design their own tapestries and embroider their own memories. Little girls learning life lessons from big girls.

Queen for a Moment

The sixteen contestants all waited nervously. Some were giggling. One was preoccupied with a microscopic thread on her dress. The others were moistening their lips and waving and smiling at relatives and friends.

When two other judges and I entered the decorated room, there was an immediate hush. Everybody seemed to be watching us, trying to read our faces. We had tallied the numbers and determined the winner. Fred, the emcee, who had been teasing, bantering, and flirting with each contestant, suddenly became very serious and intent. In his Bob Barker voice, he reminded the contestants, "Regardless of the results, each one of you is beautiful. You all deserve to wear the crown and the title."

Suddenly I was no longer a responsible, grown-up judge; I was fifteen years old again.

Homecoming queens were the epitome of success, glamour, and popularity when I was growing up in the South. By the end of September or early October, the rituals began. High school home-rooms selected their representatives for the homecoming court. A handful of girls would be ecstatic. The rest of us glanced down to hide any trace of disappointment that might show on our faces. After the announcement, I couldn't wait to find my best friend, Marsha, to discuss who we thought should have been on the ballot. Within days, the student body voted for the prettiest, most popular, most beloved girl on campus.

Preparing for homecoming lasted several weeks. A flurry of activities surrounded the event. Dresses had to be fitted, escorts selected, parade convertibles secured, and dance dates determined. But the most important activity of homecoming centered around the design and building of the class floats.

Those floats were crucial to the success of homecoming. Flat-bed trailers, borrowed from local farmers, were hidden away in barns or empty warehouses waiting to be transformed into homecoming floats. Each class had a float and each float had a theme. There was always one that sported a gray tombstone spray-painted with the initials R.I.P. (Rest In Peace) and the opposing team's name. Typically, one float sported a goal post and rowdy riders leading cheers. No matter what the theme, they all had one thing in common: the dominance of the Cass High Colonels over the homecoming rivals.

During the week of homecoming, all the students gathered together at their respective float sites and the rites of passage began. Because it was after school hours, girls could wear pants, peddle pushers, shorts, or jeans. School letter jackets were passed between the team heroes and their latest crushes. Attire was as carefully selected for these events as for the homecoming sock-hop.

No matter where the floats were being assembled, the atmosphere was the same. Sawdust covered the floor and extension cords were strung from a plug for radios and extra lighting. Coke bottles, Tootsie Roll Pop sticks, and bubble gum wrappers littered the floor. The mood was set: fun, school spirit, and potential romances. Freshmen and sophomores were serious about their chance to win the first-place prize. Juniors and seniors were serious about appearing aloof, but still pulling off a float that would not embarrass their class.

Somehow, it all eventually came together. Somehow, somebody in the class would cut through the chaos and decide on a theme and design. The boys nailed chicken wire to the flatbed trailer, creating a mesh skirt that hung to the floor. Each hole was filled with white paper napkins. Then cardboard letters were stapled and glued on. Later, we became more sophisticated and discovered colored *pomps* (small squares of tissue paper). The designated message or theme could be woven into the background.

We girls giggled, whispered, and located the closest bathroom. Boys swaggered, talked about cars and engines, and bragged about the Cass High Colonels kicking butt on Friday night.

Since it was early in the school year, new flirtations began—a little push off the float, or a helping hand to get onto the float, or a high-pitched "Help! Can you hold this for me?" and on and on until suddenly dates for the dance were secure. Or, in the case of younger couples, dance partners were guaranteed.

One question that always hung in the air, though, was, "Will this float be finished in time for the parade on Friday?"

Somehow, between Thursday afternoon and midnight, the floats were finished. Bragging rights about the best float subsided as everyone realized that it was an achievement just to have a float, best or not! Spies reported about the other class floats and students debated whether a guard was needed to protect a float from vandalism. The chaperones quickly dispelled this notion, and finally, it was time to go home and prepare for the big day and the big game.

The homecoming parade took precedence over everything in our small town. The local police blocked off the parade route, and parents and younger kids lined the street. The band was heard blocks away, drums declaring the marching cadence. Cheerleaders wore corsages made of giant gold or white chrysanthemums and decorated with the pipe-cleaner letters, CHS.

Majorettes shed their jackets at the last minute and began to dance and twirl down Main Street. The new tassels on their boots had been ordered especially for homecoming. The floats arrived with some anxious students running alongside trying to make last minute repairs. Tissue paper soon littered the streets as floats blew in the wind and the not-so-careful stuffing job came undone.

And then, either on a float designed for regal attention—or on the back of a shiny convertible—the queen contestants and the court arrived. Beautiful girls with up-swept hairdos and beautiful gowns—gowns with flowing taffeta and lace crinoline and gowns fitted with sequins, satin, and slits. Empire-waist gowns with demure bows under youthful bosoms. Full-skirted gowns clinched tightly to show off tiny waists, crinoline petticoats, and dyed-to-match satin shoes. To add even more elegance, each girl wore a pair of long, over-the-elbow white gloves. Confections of innocence, youth, and crowd-pleasing smiles and waves.

After the parade, everyone rushed about getting ready for the football game, the dance, and maybe even the parking that would take place in the old cemetery or out by the old go-cart race track.

During halftime of the big game, the band presented a special show. The members marched in rhythm while forming the design of a crown on the field. The announcer called the name of each girl and she had her moment in the spotlight—in front of friends, parents, and some little girls dreaming of becoming a queen.

Finally, the name of the winner was announced. Squeals, hugs, tears, and a shaky hand attaching the crown that usually refused to stay in place. Everyone stepped back to pay tribute to the most beautiful girl in the world, at least for that moment. And all but one girl was bravely swallowing the lump of disappointment in her throat. Marsha and I immediately compared notes on who we thought should have won. It helped us be less disappointed that we weren't part of the magic on the football field.

As the years rolled by, I realized that I would probably never be the homecoming queen. With each nomination and vote, I held my breath, caught between the fear of disappointment and the fear of victory. I silently calmed myself when my name wasn't called, vowing that nobody would ever see how much it mattered. I tried to hate the winners and look for things about them not to like.

What I realized much later on is that the winners were usually the girls in school who didn't try so hard to be liked, to fit in. They were natural, comfortable in their skin, and able to celebrate their youth. As I matured, I recalled those measurements of success: Homecoming Queen; Miss This or That; Cheerleader; Majorette; Star Student, Star Player. All measures of merit, but not measures of self-worth.

A couple of years before we married, Randy and I were riding with our friend, Wendy Bell, in the countryside in his old

1968 Cutlass convertible, top down. Wendy laughed about how she rode in one just like it during her high school homecoming parade. I shared my tale of missed opportunities. Randy and Wendy gave each other a wink and suggested I get up on the back and ride now. So I did. I sat on the back of the convertible, blew kisses, and waved, just like a real queen. As I started to get down, they encouraged me to continue for another mile or so. Little did I realize that there was a carload of Sunday drivers watching the shenanigans of a wannabe homecoming queen! But I was finally the queen and having fun—and I didn't care who watched!

In 1999, those memories seemed to flash through my mind in a matter of minutes. Startled, I realized that now I was one of three judges choosing a queen. The outcome of the event was partially in my hands. As the emcee announced the winner, I looked around the room and wished that I could quickly change my vote. Was number 10 more deserving than number 16? Should I have been more considerate of the age of number 8? Or a little less critical of number 3?

Miss Convalescent Home was finally announced. The ladies squealed, tears filled a few eyes, and shaky hands attached the crown that didn't want to stay in place. Everyone stepped back to give the Queen a moment in the spotlight—a moment in her life.

As I watched from the judge's table, I felt myself struggling. A lump rose in my throat as I recalled my own quest for the jeweled crown. Was life teaching me another lesson? Could I celebrate myself and not wait for three judges—or a student body—to permit me to feel wonderful, beautiful, and deserving? Then I wondered if the contestants knew this lesson.

But in the next moments, I realized that these 70, 80, and 90-year olds already knew that it was just a pageant after all. And that the winner of *Miss Convalescent Home* was simply a Queen For A Moment. They were far wiser than I had been!

The Jeanetic Code

I hate trying on jeans.

There's something disheartening about standing in a store and sorting through the options of jeans. Slim fit — I don't even pretend those might fit. Comfort fit—what that really means is that there is more room in the hips and thighs, but they will probably still be too tight.

Low-cut waist, just like in college when we wore our jeans below our belly button, much to our parents' chagrin. Wide-leg, bootleg, tapered leg. Five-pocketed, rivet-pocketed. Front-zippered, side-zippered, or elastic in the waist.

Such a challenge. Made even worse by the picture I have in my mind. For I still visualize myself as a college coed. Slimmer hips, narrower waist, fewer pounds. I'm always shocked when the image in the mirror doesn't match the one in my mind.

And even though I hate it, trying on jeans is a nostalgic event.

I didn't really start wearing blue jeans until I was in college. It was the fall of 1969, and the girls at Samford University in Birmingham, Alabama, could not wear jeans or any kind of slacks. We had to wear dresses to class, and afterward we could change into pantsuits. Pantsuits arrived on the fashion scene about the same time as double-knit polyester fabric. The *suit* was actually a pair of pants paired with a matching tunic top.

Samford University sits on the side of a mountain just south of Birmingham, Alabama. Most of the students are second-generation students, coming from preaching and teaching families throughout the South. The school was steeped in tradition.

Each spring, parents came to watch *Step-Sing*, an annual competitive musical event that was originally held on the steps of the Student Union Building. Students attended Convocation in the chapel every Wednesday morning, the Baptist Student Union was the biggest club on campus, and girls were required to live in the dorm and adhere to a mandatory study period. Each dorm had a housemother and a hall monitor for every floor. Their jobs were to make sure that we didn't miss the 10:00 curfew—11:00 on weekends!

But the times were a'changing. At other campuses, dorms were going coed, students were organizing sit-ins and peace rallies, and coeds were wearing whatever they wanted to! By 1972, the world was creeping up the mountainside of Samford University like kudzu vine over the South in the summertime . . . slowly but steadily changing the landscape. Even music was rebellious and the war in Viet Nam was a hot topic at every cafeteria meal.

Campuses like Samford are filled with legends, so my class created our own. It had to do with changing the dress code. The story has it that a coed wore a pants suit to class one day. When she was reminded of the *no pants rule*, she simply excused herself, took off the pants, and returned to class wearing the tunic top. The top was as long as the mini-skirts that were then the fashion rage—even at Samford.

A legend was born and the dress code changed.

Nonetheless, it wasn't until the end of my Samford years that jeans were allowed in the classroom. I had gone through my own metamorphosis. I was no longer trying to find a preacher to marry (much to my parents' disappointment). Instead, I was dating Turner, the "most hippie" guy on campus. His jeans were tattered, his bell-bottoms the widest, and his hair the shaggiest. Mama said he looked like a shaggy dog, but that didn't bother me. I was as close to rebellious as I would ever get, and I was enjoying it. And I was having a wonderful time!

It was then that I set out to search for my own perfect pair of jeans. In the life I was leaving behind, I would have gone to Belk's or Rich's or some other respectable department store. Not now, though. I headed out to the Army/Navy store, to the Jeans Depot, to the Merry-Go-Round and other establishments catering to my generation's new lifestyle and attitudes.

It took all day to find the perfect pair . . . a pair that sat really low on my hips, bell-bottoms as wide as my foot was long, and 3-inch belt loops. I was almost ready to go, but not quite.

The next step was to make the jeans uniquely mine. First they had to be washed several times to get rid of the sizing, fade them a little, and make them just a bit snugger. Then the personalization began. I used needle and colored thread and all the sewing skills learned from Miss Corinne. On the side of one leg, I stitched a row of yellow and orange flowers trailing a green vine. They matched the ring I had made out of beads and thin wire. On the other pants leg, about mid-thigh, I drew and embroidered a beautiful rainbow.

The real finishing touch, however, was a 4-inch red heart. It was artfully sewn right in the center back of the seat of the jeans (what was I thinking?). Nobody else had a pair any finer even at the Allman Brothers concerts, the Frisbee throws in the park, or the *hanging out* that was quickly becoming the dating game of the '70s.

Jeans continue to be my staple wardrobe. Styles changed, sizes changed, shades of blue changed. But my love affair with my denim jeans never faded away. I created a purse out of an old pair. I pieced together faded jeans to make a halter-top. And for about 15 years, I kept 4-inch squares cut from my old jeans with the intent of someday creating a handmade quilt. The squares stayed in the bottom of my trunk along with a set of drumsticks from an Allman Brothers concert and my old college jeans, red heart and all, until . . . well, I don't really remember what happened to these once-treasured pieces of myself.

As my life took different turns, somehow the jeans, drum sticks, and patches of denim were left by the wayside.

Today my trunk holds the sequined jeans that Randy gave me for my 35th birthday . . . right next to the first pair of jeans I bought for my grandson, size nine-months. Neither he nor I will wear those jeans again!

In my closet, I have my *fat jeans,* my work jeans (a collage of all the paint colors in my house) and my riding jeans, with enough room to be able to lift into the saddle of the horse. I have my everyday jeans, my dressy jeans, and my cut-offs. And I have a pair of jeans that I plan to wear again just as soon as I lose eight more pounds.

But most of all, I have my memory jeans. They're not in the back of the closet or the bottom of a trunk. They are stashed away in the recesses of my mind—embroidered jeans, designer jeans, work jeans and Levi's. And the pair I wore to my 10th-year high school class reunion. I remember that even after living on water and lettuce for two weeks, I still had to lie down on the bed to zip those suckers up—but they sure did look good!

Blue jeans are woven into my wardrobe tapestry across the years of my life. Taking me through college, into the wild west of my 20s, and back to the South. My life is a clothesline of jeans . . . a collage of the stories . . . a sign of the times.

What a delicious secret code the jeans and I share!

A Woman of Independent Means

I never really understood independent women until I met Millie Johnson. She was born in 1900, which made her "as old as the century." We were almost birthday twins, born one day and fifty-one years apart. But I always wanted to believe that it was a kindred spirit that made us so much alike. Millie actually lived the pioneer life I only dreamed about.

As a fifth grader, my favorite books were about life on the frontier. I sat and daydreamed for hours about living the life of the *Little House on the Prairie* children or one of the many daring and adventurous women of early American history. Millie Johnson re-awakened my early pioneer fantasies of a woman traveling across the American continent to live in the wild, wild west.

I met Millie in the mountains of New Mexico, where my friends and I hung out on weekends and just kicked back. It was the mid-1970s, and I had left the safety net of home and family in Georgia to move to New Mexico and find myself. Struggling with the changing times, I had one foot in the free-spirit, hippie-type world and the other foot in a more traditional world.

The cabin was on the bank of the Ute River (about the size of a large stream) in Ute Park, New Mexico. It was actually a summer area for fishing, hiking, and the simple pleasures of being in the foothills of the Rocky Mountains. We used it for the delights of winter snowfalls, telling tales in front of the rock fireplace, and singing along with Willie and Waylon and The Boys . . . and visiting with Millie.

Millie lived alone in a cabin just up the hill. Not just any cabin either. She had moved the cabin from the panhandle of Texas. Millie always prided herself on being a Texan through and through, and thought nothing of bringing a little bit of Texas with her to the New Mexico mountains. Her only companion in the two-bedroom log cabin was a calico cat named Callie, each of them trying to be a little more persnickety than the other.

Although Millie was petite in stature, those who knew her would tell you she was more than a handful. That might have been the reason she never married. This is not to say that Millie was a spinster—far from it.

There was nothing about Millie to make us feel that men had ever slighted her. She had photographs to attest to a long-ago courtship with an ace reporter in Washington, DC. In one photograph, petite Millie dangled from his arm as he raced for a historic interview with Lindbergh after the famous return trip across the Atlantic.

Occasionally there were references to a *friend* whose sick wife kept him tied to her for forty years or so, but Millie never talked much about a real love in her life. However, she did talk enough to let us know that there had been plenty of opportunities for lovers and she was the one who held them at bay.

Even into her late seventies, Millie wasn't immune to the

attentions of men. In fact, she always manipulated the seating arrangements, putting herself in the middle of the *boys* in our group. Every night before we parted company, she asked one of the guys to rub a little liniment on her shoulders—for her arthritis, of course.

And then, off came the pastel sweater, and her bony fingers unbuttoned her blouse with the Peter Pan collar. Suddenly, there was Millie in her undershirt (ordered annually from the JC Penney catalog). She handed the liniment to her chosen masseur, and with glaring eyes, dared anyone to make an uncomely comment. The obliging male cautiously massaged Millie's shoulders (just past her collarbone) and respectfully teased Millie about whether she was sure enough liniment had been rubbed in. Millie responded with a little coyness that delighted everyone, especially Millie.

Afterward, the selected male was teased about the flirtation with Millie. There were suggestions of Millie's physical likeness to a certain libidinous Granny character of *Playboy* fame!

Being in such a reclusive area, Millie loved having company and loved having attention.

Only a few people lived year-round in Ute Park. In fact, the only other full-time resident I ever knew was Jack.

Jack, a bachelor, lived in his own cabin between Millie's and ours. He was Millie's self-appointed gopher and handyman, and, no matter how hard he tried, he was never able to please her.

Jack drove Millie where she needed to go. She had no car. "No need," she said. She had never learned to drive anyway, because there was always someone around willing to accommodate. Once a week or so, Jack and Millie would go to the small town of Cimarron where Millie bought her groceries, managed her banking, picked up drugstore supplies, and lectured Jack on the evils of alcohol. He usually passed his time at the Two-Headed Calf Saloon while Millie privately tended to her business.

The Two-Headed Calf Saloon was a swell place. A stuffed, two-headed calf hung just above the doorway separating the dance floor from the bar. No matter how many times I studied that calf, I never determined if it was real or just some taxidermist's idea of a joke.

Another unusual sight at the saloon was a wood inlaid picture of a beautiful Spanish girl—right in the middle of the worn dance floor. Charlie, another Ute Park loner, crafted the picture. The tones and textures of the various woods blended to give life to the mysterious senorita and speculation about what role that woman may have played in Charlie's life.

While Jack was busy complaining about Millie to his barroom buddies, she completed her shopping by buying several cartons of cigarettes. "Marlboro Lights, regular, not menthol," was the way Millie requested her smokes. She considered smoking cigarettes her only vice and she wasn't too concerned about the health hazards. "I don't inhale anyway!" she declared to anyone brave enough to mention lung disease.

Jack and Millie were like siblings—muttering to anyone and everyone about "what a pain in the ass" the other one was. Jack just didn't have enough class for Millie—after all, she not only came from Texas, but she also had Mississippi River cotton plantation blood in her body. No one was ever certain about where Jack came from, but it was evident he wasn't going to go very far.

Back at her cabin, Millie fed the local deer and wild turkeys every day. After I spent some time with her and got to know her better, Millie taught me how to be a part of the feeding ritual.

Before long, I could hold a piece of apple or bread in my hand and a deer would gently remove it. The turkeys were a little more skeptical, but eventually even they responded to the sound of the corn in the aluminum pie plate as a sign that I, too, was a friend.

When I was in the mountains, Millie replaced Jack at the drop of a hat in order to ride in my Spitfire convertible and, later, my Toyota Landcruiser. (By the way, this was the old kind of Landcruiser, not today's SUV kind!) Millie liked it best when we were riding in the convertible with the top down. She would wrap a scarf around her tightly knotted silver bun and reminisce about days with her ace reporter.

During these rides, I believe Millie mostly wanted to be seen. Wherever she saw anyone she might remotely know, she would instruct me to "Give them the horn." Then she would casually acknowledge the person with a smug nod and cocky little grin.

Millie was pretty modern for her age. And although she didn't pry too much into the sleeping arrangements at the cabin down the hill, I didn't ever get the idea that she approved of unmarried people cohabiting. She always offered me a bed at her house if there weren't enough to go around at the cabin. However, her favorite bit of gossip was about one of her summer neighbors, a couple about her age. She took a lot of pride in introducing me to them and I assumed they were married. But one afternoon Millie whispered to me, "No, they're not married. Their children didn't approve, so to teach the children a lesson, the couple just lives together." She always got a kick out of repeating that bit of gossip!

Millie had a funny little habit of pursing her lips into a perfect circle, raising her eyebrows, and exclaiming "Oh?" at particular times. I later realized that her "Oh?" was her response to things she was not too clear about or to indiscreet subjects. Her voice would rise just enough to suggest surprise or questioning. How I loved to hear that "Oh?" I always had to suppress giggles if any of my friends were around.

Unique expressions were Millie's forte. Always a great Texan lady, Millie used more genteel phrases than the average person. The funniest was her unusual term for passing gas. She would always look demure and say, "Excuse me, I *fluffed.*" Don't ask me why she put it that way, I never asked.

She and I had a special bond—sisters in the mountains— Millie in her seventies, I in my twenties. I liked it best in the summertime when I went to Ute Park for a week or two at the time by myself. We had our routine. We sat at her small kitchen table and discussed events of the world and of the heart. I loved the three-tine silver forks we used for eating. They were the first I had ever seen. The tines were sharp, the silver softly mellowed with age and use.

We always sat at the table for our meals—sandwiches and salad for lunch, a meat, vegetable, and fruit for dinner. Afterward we sipped coffee in delicate porcelain cups and ate a small bit of cake or maybe two cookies. As I washed the dishes, Millie would give the chokecherry bush outside her door a sip of water, then sit in her favorite rocker in front of the fire and reach for her Marlboro Lights (regular, not menthol), never inhaling.

After the dishes were done, we would take right up with our conversations about men, politics, family, history, and religion (she was Methodist, I was Southern Baptist), until another day had passed in Ute Park.

I depended on Millie to help me try to straighten out my confusion about relationships, love, and marriage. I wanted to be an independent woman, but found my happiness more and more dependent on the attention of boyfriends. I wanted to be my own person, just like Millie. I had a hard time expressing myself around my peers. I continually swallowed my opinions, waiting to see what others thought first.

But with Millie, I could talk about anything, and by talking I felt that I kept my foot a little more grounded in the traditions of my youth. Probably because of Millie's influence, I moved home to Georgia in 1978 after Daddy got really sick. And I only saw her one more time.

In 1979, Jack found Millie dead at the cabin; it was a heart attack. He mourned and made some phone calls. And I mourned.

The final arrangements were fitting. Millie was not one to leave the mountains of New Mexico, except one rare time for her great niece's wedding. But when it was time for her to go to her final home, she had made arrangements to go back to Texas. By the time I got in touch with her niece, Mildred Ann, Millie's possessions had been moved to Texas, her cabin had been sold, and except for her spirit and Jack's heart, Millie was gone from Ute Park.

I have always been disappointed that I didn't have a special memento of my time with Millie. But sometimes, as I sit down to eat a lunch-time sandwich and salad with my own three-tine fork, I think of Millie and our special time together. The memory makes my face and my heart smile.

I'd love to be able to share with Millie what has happened since her death. I'd tell her how I've resolved relationships, love, and marriage. I'd proudly let her know that I have learned to speak my own mind. I can just hear her questioning "Oh?" about some of my decisions, but I think, for the most part, she would offer an affirming, "Ah!"

The Haul of Fame

S ometimes it's difficult to protect people from what they
don't need to know. Such is the case of the summer my
cousin Martha Jean and I ran a yard clean-up business.

Since we were school teachers and single, there never seemed
to be enough money to make ends meet. I generally ran out of
money long before the next payday, so I often found myself
working summer jobs to supplement my teaching salary.

Being an outdoors-type person, I learned at a young age that
I liked doing yard work and housework much better than I liked
being cooped up in an office all day or serving cocktails and food
from mid-afternoon to late evening for the promise of a tip.

Our adventure started the summer cousin Martha Jean and
I helped her daddy, Uncle Leslie, paint his house. I was pretty
brave and not afraid of heights, so I was the one who climbed the
tall ladder onto the roof, lay on my belly, and reached over the
edge of the roof to paint the cornice boards. Martha Jean stood
on the ground below cheering me on. Uncle Leslie stood on the
ground below holding his breath. When I climbed down the
ladder at the end of the day, Martha Jean and I talked about how

much fun we'd had, that it hardly seemed at all like work!

Within days, Martha Jean and I decided to run a yard-cleaning and house-painting service. We knew how to cut grass, trim bushes, paint, and do all sorts of other odd jobs. We figured we could borrow the riding mower and all the tools we would need from our parents' well-stocked tool sheds. And Daddy had already given me full use of his pick-up truck, Old Blue: standard on the column, no air-conditioning, and no radio.

We ran an ad in the local paper, and on the first day it appeared, we got our first call. Someone living in a country house needed some rubbish hauled away. Not knowing what we were getting into, we naively agreed to accept this, our first job. When we arrived, we discovered we had to pull up old carpets from a floor. Moldy, mildewy carpets. YUCK! Not only were they smelly, they were extremely heavy! And they had to be taken to a landfill thirty miles away. Thank goodness Daddy's truck was filled with gas when we borrowed it.

Our next job was out in the country too. A young bride wanted to surprise her husband with a freshly mowed yard and a little bit of cleaning up around the house. We were excited to have more work and this sounded more like what we had in mind when we ran the ad. We could cut grass especially well with Uncle Leslie's riding lawn mower. However, when we arrived, we learned that the main job would be the *little bit* of cleaning up around the house. It was a lot of cleaning up and another pretty disgusting job of picking up century-old trash and debris and hauling it the same thirty miles away.

Finally, we landed the kind of job we were looking for—mowing, clearing, and trimming a yard that had been neglected all spring and summer. It was in town and there didn't appear to be any yucky stuff to take to the dump.

We began early in the morning and were so busy that we didn't notice the traffic on the main road slowing down to take a look at two healthy and tanned yard girls going about their work in shorts and T-shirts. At noon, we took a break to drink our R.C. Colas and eat our Moon Pies—Martha and I were determined to act the part of traditional laborers in the South, even if we didn't look the part!

We agreed to do the job for twenty dollars. But before we even worked an hour, we knew we had under priced the job again. No wonder we were getting to be so popular! However, we felt this job would be great for referrals, so we continued to work as if we were getting paid three times as much.

When the homeowner arrived, he was amazed at the difference we had made in his yard. We beamed. He confirmed our price and explained he would be back in a few minutes with cash to pay us. When he returned, he placed a ten-dollar bill in each of our scratched and grimy hand. He then told us he had a bonus for us. We thought it was because of our exceptional work. Later we found out it was because he realized we had seriously undercharged him!

He opened his trunk and cheerfully pointed to two cases of beer. That was our bonus! We could barely hide our dismay! We were caught in an unusual situation. That summer, Martha Jean and I were both living with our parents. I did not even have a car with me and used Daddy's truck for transportation. Martha's car was in the shop, so she was driving her mama's car.

The challenge we now faced was what to do with the beer. Neither set of our parents approved of alcohol in any form. They prided themselves in never allowing even a beer in their homes. They felt their influence on children was too powerful to expose us to the dangers of drinking.

We knew this was going to be a dilemma. Finally, we left with the beer in the back of Daddy's truck and secretly transferred it to the trunk of Aunt Lucile's car. We phoned Martha Jean's older brother, Butch. We knew he'd be happy to help us get rid of our *bonus*. Our plan was to meet at Martha Jean's parents' home and discreetly transfer the beer from the trunk of Aunt Lucile's car to Butch's waiting ice chests.

On the appointed day, at the appointed hour, everything was set. Martha Jean and I were there with the beer stashed in the trunk of the car. Thank goodness Aunt Lucile was busy downstairs doing laundry and was not likely to notice anything unusual going on. Cousin Butch drove up and parked across the road from the house so as not to attract any unnecessary attention. He opened the trunk of his car for us as we quickly opened the trunk of Aunt Lucile's car. Martha and I each grabbed a case of beer and scurried down the driveway to the get-away car.

Just about the time we were halfway there, Uncle Leslie unexpectedly rounded the corner, turning into the drive. Like two deer caught in head lights, we instantly froze and then simultaneously turned around and rushed back to the open trunk of Aunt Lucile's car. As we furtively moved across the front of the house, the door opened wide and, much to our dismay, there stood Aunt Lucile in the doorway.

Faces red, with guilt popping out over us like adolescent pimples, we thrust the beer back into the trunk and tried to look natural. Uncle Leslie took one look and knew something was going on. We hemmed. We hawed. We stuttered. We tried to slip casually away, but too late. We were caught red-handed with beer in Aunt Lucile's car!

In that moment, we could hardly understand how things

had gone so awry. We were trying to protect our parents from something we found ourselves innocently caught in. We had gone to great lengths to be gracious about the beer and at the same time honor our family values. Before long, we were confessing the entire incident and assuring everyone that Butch was only trying to help us in our dilemma.

I decided at that moment that sometimes it is just too much work to try to protect everybody all the time. Amazingly, no one was offended by our beer bonus. In fact, our parents took much delight in retelling the story time after time, much to our chagrin.

And finally, when I was about forty years old, I did have a glass of wine with dinner in front of Mama. She didn't approve. But then, I didn't expect her to.

Bought the Farm

Y ou never know what you can do until you just do it.

Cousin Martha Jean and I proudly showed off the *For Sale* house we had just discovered. Our mamas looked as if they would cry. Our daddies just looked tired. Martha Jean and I were so excited that we barely noticed their reactions! We anxiously explained to our parents what a *find* the house was. It was a real farmhouse, over 100 years old, and just outside of town on three acres. Why, the property even included a wonderful pecan orchard on two of the three acres. Behind the house was a three-holer (outhouse), an old smokehouse, and a barn with lots of afternoon light streaming through the well-worn boards.

On the day we showed our parents the farmhouse, Martha Jean and I were kinda nervous that they might miss all the good stuff because they were too busy looking at all the junk abandoned by the last renter. So we kept pointing out feature after glorious feature. The ceilings were still twelve feet high even after being lowered; the bedrooms were very, very large; there were lots of windows in every room; and most exciting of all, a wonderful porch ran around half the house. We envisioned ourselves sitting in rocking chairs and on porch swings. Our parents envisioned us trying to stay warm on cold winter nights and painting and remodeling for months.

We were like Lucy and Ethel trying to convince Ricky and Fred that our newest escapade was the best idea ever! We knew this was going to be a hard sell.

Our parents immediately saw the need for adequate plumbing. In our excitement, we didn't realize that the sewage was discreetly piped out into the pecan orchard and we would have to put in a septic tank immediately. They also knew that the one fuse supplying electricity to the house would make it necessary for us to rewire the house. And they knew that the two old gas space heaters would not keep us warm in the winter.

They didn't appreciate the fine living-room light fixture— a gas-burning lamp from another era that had been redesigned into an electrical light. Looking back, I don't think our parents were so fond of that era.

While they saw carpets worn so thin that they would literally have to be scraped off the floors, we saw finished wooden dance floors. We proudly showed them the antique pieces the owner was leaving us—a cherry-stained wardrobe that would be exquisite once it was refinished. And in the kitchen, there was an antique cupboard complete with glass doors and flour bins that pulled out. They could only see that the entire kitchen would have to be gutted, refurbished, and plumbed.

Once we envisioned wonderful summer parties on the porch and the fun winter nights in the cozy living room, we couldn't be dissuaded. In spite of their disapproval, we marched ourselves right down to the bank and took out a loan to buy the house. There was a minor problem, however, when we tried to get fire insurance for the house. While we thought the tin roof over the kitchen added a charming touch, the insurance companies called the roof a fire hazard. Thank goodness, in rural Georgia, there were still insurance companies for farm folks and other imaginative people who understood the value of homes of bygone eras. We got the insurance, we got the loan, and we got the awaiting adventure.

On a beautiful, breezy October day in 1979, we moved into our house. We took pictures of ourselves as we opened the front door of *our farmhouse* for the first time. Proud owners that we were, we just then noticed that several panes of glass in the door were missing. It was also then that we discovered the door handle came off in our hand if we twisted it too hard. However, we were all excitement—all dreams, all youth, and all energy. And it turned out that the energy was a good thing! Making a hundred-year-old farmhouse habitable was hard enough, but making it livable was going to be a major undertaking.

So we began at the beginning. We weren't interested in cleaning. Martha Jean and I wanted to decorate! We planned to eventually paint Martha Jean's room green to go with her comforter and pillows, as well as an interesting art piece that an old beau had painted, but first we had to tear down a spooky closet made out of cheap paneling. Then we moved to my room, where we stripped the sagging wallpaper. Underneath the wallpaper, we discovered unpainted hardwood walls that had been built in the 1800s. The wallpaper had been hung on cheesecloth, then nailed to the walls. Through the years, the paper sagged, creating a spooky illusion in the shadows of the security light our Dads had installed in the front yard.

As friends helped Martha and me get started on our projects,

Uncle Leslie and Daddy began some minor structural renovation—like fixing the front steps and front porch so no one would fall through. Aunt Lucile dug in with both hands and started cleaning. She could take her pick of rooms to clean because every inch of the house needed a hot sudsy bath. Mama tackled the peeling red and white paint on the kitchen cupboard, but after about fifteen minutes of work, she realized there were seven more coats of oil paint underneath. She called the nearest furniture refurbishing shop and had them pick it up for refinishing. It was her house warming present to us.

That first work day seemed endless. We moved my iron bed into the front room—the same bed I had found several years before by the side of the road in rural New Mexico. The old family pump organ became the focal point of the living room. Mama, Uncle Leslie, and the rest of their siblings had grown up singing around that pump organ. We inherited a cast off refrigerator from Uncle Leslie's basement. Mama and Aunt Lucile stocked it before we could turn around. Box after box of stuff was brought in. And during the whole time, we kept on cleaning. This work and the move into the house was not going nearly as quickly as we had imagined or hoped.

At the end of the first of many full days of labor, we insisted that our parents go home without us. We were determined to sleep in our new house. We would be fine. We were not afraid. We were safe. So after the daddies installed new security locks on all the outside doors, patched the windowpanes in the front door, and left, we were finally alone. Just Martha Jean and me in our new old farmhouse!

We turned to each other as we got ready to take our showers and go to bed. I looked at Martha Jean; Martha Jean looked at me. Her brown eyes got deeper and browner, my lighter eyes got wider and wider. We talked lightly about the day, avoiding the fact that we were both just a little bit nervous about the big old house. Finally, we both took deep breaths and decided to put the cards on the table.

We were afraid. Especially of mice. We were not just afraid—we were terrified by the thought that there might even be ONE in our house. And after a day of cleaning, we knew that the place had been inhabited by those *you-know-whaties* (those were the words we used to refer to rodents).

That night, we were both afraid of what we would encounter in the dark rooms, the same rooms that were so filled with light, energy, and dreams during the day. So we devised a plan, one that would last throughout our years together. It went like this. Before we entered a room, we opened the door slightly. We reached around the corner and turned on the light. Then we stomped one foot very sharply on the floor three times. After waiting a few seconds, we figured it was safe to enter the room. We figured the light and the noise would send any uninvited visitors away.

After we made our plan, we felt better. We went to the kitchen together, reaching around the door, turning on lights, and stomping the whole way through three rooms. We got glasses of water and then we repeated the whole foot-stomping process as we went into the bathroom. While I showered, Martha sat and talked to me. Her main job, though, was to be on the lookout for anything that might try to get us. I did the same for her. As we started to go to our separate rooms, we pulled down all the shades, double-locked all the new locks, and shut all the doors except the ones between our bedrooms. We said our good nights and turned to separate rooms just as the spooky shadows began to play tricks on us. Immediately we turned back to each other and decided that it was probably a good idea to sleep in the same room this first night . . . just until we got adjusted, we said.

The next morning, after assuring our parents that we had a great night, we agreed to let them set out some mousetraps—the kind that had to be checked and dealt with. In this area, I was less brave and more fearful than Martha Jean was. I could not bear the thoughts of checking a trap. So I finally convinced Martha Jean that she was indeed the braver one. Her job was to check the trap every morning. I would wait outside the swinging door separating the kitchen from the dining room until she gave me the *all-clear* signal.

On the third day in the house, Martha Jean was screaming as she came flying out of the kitchen. Without questioning her, I dropped everything, screamed with her, and raced with her to the safety of the front porch. Martha Jean had discovered a *you-know-whatie* in the trap.

What could we do? We certainly couldn't call home and ask our parents to handle this. They were just waiting for a chance to remind us that we didn't need to live in such a place. And besides, we were in our late twenties and constantly trying to prove to our families that we were indeed mature and responsible.

Finally, after much talk on my part, Martha agreed, once again, that she was braver than I was. Armed with a large, brown paper sack and a broom, she entered the kitchen. Again, I stood just on the other side of the swinging door. As she struggled with her newfound courage, I coached her, assuring her that she could do it. She gave me a play-by-play description of her activities as she approached the task.

A shaky voice came out of the kitchen, "I'm opening the sack."

"You're doing great, Martha Jean!" I replied.

"Oh my gosh, Shirl, I don't know if I can do this."

"Yes, you can, Martha Jean. You are BRAVE!" More encouraging words came from the dining room. "Just open the cabinet door and use the broom," I said.

Martha squealed as she swept the trap into the large paper grocery bag. Then she had a momentary panic attack, and fled the kitchen and ran into the dining room.

I used some more encouraging words until finally, taking a deep breath, Martha Jean went back into the kitchen.

"Oh Shirl, I'm picking up the sack," she wailed. I could hear her cross the floor toward the back screened door.

I was still her coach. "Martha, you're doing great! You are SO brave."

As she went into the yard, I scuttled through the kitchen to the back stoop to continue cheering. She tossed the sack, contents and all, into a pit that was used to burn household garbage. She turned around and then literally flew to catch up with me as I ran again to the safety of the front porch. We were exhausted. We were spent. And we were so proud that we had dealt with our first house problem bravely.

That afternoon, our parents stopped by to help out some more. One of them noticed the missing trap and asked where it was. We proudly told them that we had taken care of it. It NEVER occurred to us to empty and recycle the trap. We were informed that there was a good chance that there were more mice . . . another thought that had not yet occurred to us.

We immediately phoned the local pest-control service for a price quote. As we struck a bargain, we explained that in no uncertain terms did we expect to EVER see a rodent or signs of a rodent in our house again. Then we got a cat. It was a small price to pay for peace of mind and a good night's sleep in our own beds.

While living in the farmhouse, Martha Jean and I learned more handywoman skills. We learned to fix plumbing, drive a back-hoe, and hammer a nail. We learned to hang sheet rock and hang wallpaper, and we soon knew the value of a good trim brush. We learned how to *pull* electrical wire, measure twice, insulate, and to use an electric saw and drill.

We spent many evenings sipping ice-cold tea while rocking on our front porch. We planned parties, our weddings, and a great future in that old farmhouse. We hosted a Plantation Party, complete with women in hooped skirts, men in Confederate uniforms, and mint juleps on the veranda.

We entertained school kids, family kids, uncles and aunts, cousins, and Sunday School classes. We hosted great Saturday night dances.

We planted a garden and canned and froze vegetables. We picked blackberries and made jam. We made ice cream while we watched lightning bugs.

One night we even staved off an intruder. That was the night we had to decide which one of us would actually pull the trigger of the small handgun that Uncle Leslie gave us. Thank goodness, we didn't have to find out who would do it. The *intruder* left before we had to decide. He was picked up a few minutes later by the Deputy Sheriff. He was lost, inebriated, and cold. No threat at all to anything other than our nerves!

Martha Jean married in 1980 and moved away. After she left, sometimes I lived alone, and sometimes I lived with roommates. However, in 1986, I finally decided to sell the farmhouse. It just wasn't the same without Martha Jean. Together, Martha Jean and I had one final party, danced one last dance on the hardwood floors, and rocked one more time on the front porch. And the next morning, before we cleaned up, we opened the kitchen door, reached around the corner, turned on the light, and stomped our feet one last time.

We left that farmhouse with a trunk full of memories, irreplaceable photographs, and a lifelong connection. We celebrate birthdays, holidays and sometimes sad days together. We're best friends and favorite cousins. We still take turns being the hero and the cheerleader in our projects and schemes, always looking for one more adventure! And we still are Lucy and Ethel!

The Weak Before

Once Martha married and moved away from the farm house, I rattled around in it by myself for about a year before life took a new turn for me.

It was a Friday afternoon and another year of teaching school was over. In one more week—June 6, 1981—I was finally going to get married! My fiancé, Richard, and I had dated for eight years and he would be leaving that very afternoon to drive from New Mexico to begin married life with me in Georgia.

I was looking over the display of wedding gifts spread throughout three rooms of the old farmhouse. Just a year before, Martha Jean had displayed her wedding gifts in the very same rooms. My excitement was mounting.

I received the usual wedding gifts: place settings of *good* and *everyday* china; nesting Tupperware and casserole dishes; matching *His* and *Her* towels and pillowcases. Then there were the special wedding gifts: pewter candlesticks from out west; a handmade tea pitcher crafted by a potter from Cassville, Georgia; the depression-glass cake plate from Miss Reba, and the wedding night negligees from my girlfriends. The *Bride's Gift Registry* documented each gift, the sender, and the status of writing the thank-you notes.

It was a wonderful day that early summer. The weather was warm, with a soft, fresh breeze blowing through the open windows of the house. I went out to the porch swing just to sit and take it all in. The shiny, dark green leaves of the magnolia tree reflected the sun with diamond-like brilliance. The creamy colored blossoms, at different stages of opening, looked like dancing girls. Some were still tightly closed like a ballerina on her toes. Other blossoms opened wide like Cinderella's ball gown. The hydrangea bush next to the porch was almost bent to the ground with the weight of the large, blue clusters of flowers. Each one looked like the top of a huge blueberry snow cone.

Magnificent blossoms would be at their peak just in time for the wedding. Everything was unfolding according to my plan. The magnolia blossoms and leaves would fill heart-shaped frames that would sit on the church altar, just below the candelabras. The hydrangeas would be included in the bridesmaids' and the bridal bouquets. The plans were simple, yet so beautiful.

The magic of my reverie was interrupted by the ringing phone. Reluctantly leaving my dreams of wedding days and honeymoon nights, I walked into the house and picked up the receiver. I was halfway expecting the local jewelry store to announce a delivery of more *good* china and crystal. The minute I said, "Hello," I sensed the call was about something much more important than china or crystal.

It was Richard. I knew before any words were spoken that something was wrong. "Shirley, I don't know how to tell you this except just tell you. I can't go through with this wedding. I'm not coming to Georgia." And then he added, "I hope this doesn't cause you too many problems."

My heart began pounding in my chest! My temples began a faint, yet growing, throb. My eyes lost all focus except for the bridal registry. In a flash, I was already penning the notes to friends and family that would accompany the return of the gifts. My stomach was recoiling at the satisfaction that some people would feel from this failure in my life. Suddenly I was suspicious of everyone I knew. And I was angry.

Shame and humiliation washed over me as I listened. And then I quickly replied. Without letting Richard respond to my comments, I blurted out sentence after sentence. "Oh, Richard, are you sure? I mean, I guess you are sure or you wouldn't have called. Have you told your parents? Is Dick or Kevin there with you? I thought y'all were going to start driving here today. I guess you've changed your mind. Don't worry, I can take care of everything. Of course, I'll have to return all those gifts. Your parents' friends sent us the nicest pair of pewter candlesticks from . . ."

Richard interrupted me with one last comment, "Shirley, I'm sorry. But I think this is the best thing for both of us."

I feebly replied, "Of course, I understand. It's much better to know this now, than after the wedding," followed by an "Oh, don't worry about me. I'll be fine . . . Goodbye."

As I hung up the phone, the self-talk escalated.

"Fine? This is just about as fine as being kicked in the chest by a horse. About as fine as being abandoned by my parents. About as fine as telling everybody they were right, and that you weren't the kind of guy who wanted to get married and settle down anyway. Fine!"

As I moved through a daze, I found myself talking as though Richard were in the room.

"Right now, I don't know if I want to slap you as hard as I can and leave an imprint on your cheek as visible as the imprint you have just left on my heart, or if I want to find a comforting place in your arms with my head against your chest and believe that somehow everything will soon be okay."

I was too confused to think clearly. To know what to do next.

Finally, I picked up the phone and called my friend, Ann. She was the wedding director and had coached me on social protocol so far. Besides, she could tell her husband to stop working on the heart-shaped frames for the magnolia blossoms. They wouldn't be needed, I told her. After a brief conversation, Ann knew I needed more than etiquette advice. She insisted on coming right over.

As I waited for Ann, I moved from the living room, with those wedding gifts glaring at me, to the porch where the magnolia blossoms and hydrangeas seemed to mock me.

Why didn't I tell the truth? Why didn't I angrily explain to Richard that this kind of hurt was not fair? Why did I let this moment define me instead of my defining this moment? Why did I stand there desperately wishing he would call back? Why did I want to figure out what *I* had done wrong and then fix it so we could go on?

And why didn't I listen to the gnawing in my gut instead of listening to my heart? I knew there was some validity in his decision. He was not ready to commit to the relationship. Deep down, I think I had always known that.

Ann arrived and quietly comforted me while I mourned and rationalized in the same breath.

Then the phone rang again. I was surprised to hear Dick's voice, Richard's lifelong friend. Dick said he didn't think Richard had meant what he said. It was probably just pre-wedding panic. Maybe I should put everything on hold for the afternoon while they sorted things through as only men could do.

I don't remember if it was a minute—or an hour. But I can promise you it seemed like a whole lifetime before the phone rang again. This time it was Richard.

He started, "Shirley, I guess I was just a little nervous."

I held my breath as he continued, "We're packing the car and heading out. Dick, Kevin, and I will be driving *The Bomb* (the old rattletrap of a car that was their pride and joy) and pulling the Jeep behind us. We should be there by Monday night or Tuesday morning. My folks will be getting there Thursday. Is everything ready for that dinner that Mom and Dad are supposed to give after the rehearsal?"

And just like that, my life turned around again.

I started breathing again and reassured him, "It's okay, I understand." With a nervous laugh, I continued, "After all, you've been a bachelor for 35 years. It's probably normal to panic."

Quickly, I continued to encourage him, "Don't worry, everything is in order for the rehearsal dinner on Friday night." And I finished off with, "See you Monday or Tuesday. You guys have fun, but be careful! Bye!"

"Whew!" I immediately said to myself. "That was a close call."

And yet, as I placed the receiver back on the phone, a part of me—the smart aleck, hurt side—wanted to say, "By the way, if you change your mind again, be sure and call."

The flood of relief was shadowed by a gnawing in my gut. Somehow, deep down, I knew that maybe the marriage shouldn't take place. If my confidence had been stronger, my pride weaker, I would have said, "Richard, you're right. This marriage will probably not work. I don't think our relationship is in the right place to start a marriage. I think I'll wait for a partner in life who is ready to be totally committed to the relationship. And I think you should wait until you are a lot more sure."

That kind of courage could have saved me from a very short, heartbreaking marriage. It could have saved me from a very pain-filled divorce. That kind of courage could have helped me make better decisions. And that kind of courage could have helped Richard do what was right for him.

But that kind of courage comes from living—from learning—from growing. That kind of courage comes from knowing that, regardless of the immediate pain, it is far better to recognize, accept, and live with the truth. That kind of courage knows that most likely you will find the truth in your gut—not in your heart.

Ride On

M y close friend, Louise, went off one weekend to find her soul.

It had been twenty-five years since we met. And over the years we've shared all sorts of girlfriend secrets. So I knew where she was headed, and why she was going. Oh, her family thought she took off on an artist's retreat to discover the secret to creating canvas masterpieces. But I knew she really went to discover the secrets of a master-filled soul.

We first met in the late 1970s when I was a physical education teacher at the local junior high school in Carrollton, Georgia. At twenty-seven and single, I still thought of myself as one of the kids—hair held back with bows or ribbons, little or no makeup, tennis shoes, and shorts or jogging suits. The gym was rather private, across the school campus from the classrooms and more traditional teaching methods.

I was a little leery when the school built a couple of classrooms along the side of the gym. Other teachers would invade my domain! I suspected they might not understand my approach to education.

Louise was hired to teach art and classes for children with special needs. She was warm, caring, brand-new to teaching, and just a bit older than I was. It turned out that she had decided to become a teacher when her marriage failed and she was raising a young daughter. One thing we had in common, though, was that we were both single women looking for love, marriage, and happiness ever after!

It wasn't long before our discussions of teaching and students turned to single-girl intimacies and I started calling her *Weezie*. She listened for hours as I lamented over the fact that my boyfriend, Richard, didn't pay me enough attention. We lived in different parts of the country and he couldn't decide whether or not to make the relationship permanent or even exclusive. Every day I would whine about my dilemma. I just couldn't decide whether to end the relationship in favor of a potentially healthier one, or keep waiting for the timing to be right with Richard.

Weezie always seemed to be able to give the right advice— even when I didn't expect it.

Once, returning to school after a date with a guy named Tom, I began to talk seriously with her about the discontent in my heart. I shared with her that Tom suspected I had a few hang-ups about life and relationships. He added that I might benefit from some professional counseling. He told me this in the most caring way, making it hard to ignore his suggestion. Instead of assuring me that I was just fine, Louise said, "I think Tom's right. You could probably use some professional help. I highly recommend Fred Richards."

To say that I was shocked was an understatement. And, like most people I knew, I thought psychologists and counselors were for crazy people! I had expected Weezie to confirm my thinking that I was just fine! Instead, she not only supported Tom's suggestion, she immediately helped me follow through. She picked up the phone to call Fred. I was nervous . . . I was excited . . . I was timid . . . but soon I was sitting in Fred's office and he and I were beginning a lifetime relationship of sharing and caring.

As soon as I realized what a difference a listening friend could make, I started paying more attention to Louise. I had been so caught up in the drama of my own life that I had failed to recognize the discord in hers.

Like me, Louise was looking for the right relationship. And like me, she wasn't always looking in the right places. She was dating Lee, a man on the mend from a fast life with a whole lot of heavy baggage. And unlike me, Louise had a constant struggle with her weight. She had been yo-yo dieting for years and needed encouragement to stay on the healthy track.

Before long, our relationship deepened as we shared stories about our pain and joys. But most of all, we began trying to sort through things to create meaning out of the crazy kind of relationships we both tended to attract.

Soon I began to understand that this art/special education teacher was a new kind of guardian angel for my spirit. No matter what was going on, Weezie pushed me to laugh, to explore, and to live with the exuberance that was natural to me.

I finally married Richard, and when the marriage took a very bad turn, it was Weezie who stood beside me in the driveway and watched as he drove away. I thought he was just going to take a trip to visit family and friends out west. She seemed to know he wasn't coming back. She could also tell that it would be some time before I was ready to confront the inevitable. Richard was gone.

After Richard left, I rented out the farmhouse and moved into the apartment above Weezie and her adorable daughter, Sherry. We laughed. We cried. We smoked a few cigarettes. Weezie found her comfort in food. I found mine in wine. Mostly, though, we discussed the turn of events in our lives. Sherry, became *Sherry Berry*, a child who turned into the most delightful young woman a mother could have. I think she learned from our mistakes!

Weezie eventually married Lee; I continued to struggle with my own *falling apart* marriage.

She was always a little more perceptive than I was and she was right. Richard never came back. I learned to accept that in my own time. It was Weezie who first noticed that Randy Garrett, the guy dating my roommate, seemed pretty interested in me. He always invited me along on their outings so I wouldn't be home alone with a fractured heart.

Weezie loved to tease me about Randy, and I would blush and deny that there was any kind of chemistry between us. In May 1986, Randy and I were married. Weezie did not attend the wedding because she was delivering her own Garrett, the unexpected child of her second marriage! And just to set the record straight, Garrett was Weezie's maiden name . . . but no kin to Randy's branch of the Bowdon, Georgia, Garrett family.

Weezie and I were soon leading chaotic lives and somehow drifted apart. Things like that happen. Weezie was busy with her new family and I was busy being Randy's wife. She taught in a different school system and I left the teaching profession to become the director of Tanner Women's Center in Carrollton, and began pursuing my doctorate degree.

Trips to Fred were less frequent for me as Weezie and I both settled in to what I considered stable, happy homes and new careers. Living in different worlds, we eventually developed other best friends and drifted apart.

But great friendships are born of connection. And life has a great way of reminding us of that.

We both lost our jobs through circumstances that still confuse us. Weezie's best friend died of cancer and she learned first hand how short life can be. Before too long, Weezie phoned me to plan a time to get together. She came out and we spent an afternoon talking, sharing, crying, and hugging—taking up just where we'd left off a few years back.

During the past few years, Weezie has become my biggest fan—my biggest cheerleader, and I, hers. We have grown in our relationship, but probably the biggest growth has taken place in our souls.

When I wrote my very first short story, Weezie was the first to read it. She picked up the paintbrush that she had abandoned many years before and created a watercolor depicting the spirit of my story. She gave it to me as a Christmas gift, and when I opened the package, I was touched in a way I had never experienced before.

We were growing. My writing and her painting were our first steps. One stretch led to another.

Weezie began in earnest to eat healthy, exercise, and develop her art. I continued to try my hand at writing. After losing forty pounds, Weezie asked me to take her to Randy's farm to see if she could ride a horse. Riding horses was a passion of Louise's youth and she wanted to give it another try. This was to be a challenge—perhaps much more emotionally than physically. I had tears in my eyes as I watched her finally mount Oscar, our quarter horse, and ride across the pastures. Another stretch.

On the way back home that afternoon, she confessed to me that, several years ago, she had cried herself to sleep one night because she believed she was either too old or too large to ever ride a horse again.

And in another stretch, Weezie had the courage to leave the marriage that wasn't working. She knew it would be hard to raise a son through adolescence, but she also knew it was the right thing for her and Garrett.

Weezie was the first of us to turn fifty. And she threatened to do something simply outrageous, like get a tattoo. You might ask her about that when you meet her.

Through all this rebirth, Weezie shed a lot of pounds. When asked about how much weight she lost, she says, "I lost a whole person. The one that didn't fit." And if someone asks what kind of diet she went on, she likes to say, "I went on a life, not a diet."

Louise or Weezie, regardless of the name attached, the friend is the same. She went away on her artist's retreat and she discovered a few things about art. What she really learned, though, was how important she is, how unique she is, what a good soul she possesses. She also picked up some stretching exercises while away.

Through the years, I have been blessed with an abundance of girlfriends and I think Weezie is part of the reason. She taught me so much about friendship, about being a listening friend as well as a talking friend, about lending emotional support, and about never being afraid to live with natural exuberance. Most of all, she taught me how to give a friend a boost, whether it is to write a story, get a head on straight, take a stretch in life, or ride a horse. What a great world it would be if everybody had a Weezie!

Knock Your Socks Off

When I married Randy, he was single. Well, of course, he was single, but he considered himself a *bachelor*, although he had been married before and had three sons—Scott, Kevin, and Matt. And since Randy planned on remaining a bachelor for a long time, he had built himself a bachelor pad. He didn't think he was going to meet somebody like me, but he did and we did. Got married, that is.

We moved into his wonderful little bachelor pad and immediately I began to think of it as a honeymoon cottage.

I had visions of Randy and me growing old together in our cottage. And just like in the movies, we would become closer and closer as we aged. We'd get to know each other so well that we would finish sentences for each other. In fact, we might even start to look alike. (Actually, since Randy has lost most of his hair, I'm hoping this part doesn't happen!)

Anyway, I was really excited about the romantic possibilities when we married. And since I had a few weeks off from work to settle into our marriage, I decided I would become the perfect little homemaker.

At the time we married, Randy was a farmer. He had a dairy farm on the west side of Carroll County, just about forty-five minutes from our home. While Randy spent the day at the farm baling hay and milking cows, I washed his clothes, ironed his shirts, cooked his meals, and when he got home, cheerfully met him at the door with a kiss!

I spent my day looking forward to the time his truck pulled into the driveway. Before he came into the house, he would stand on the outside stoop and take off his boots, which were kinda yucky. And then he would do the most adorable thing! He would take off his socks, one at a time, and somehow they would end up together in a tight little ball. Stepping into the house, he would toss the ball of socks across the foyer, over the counter, through the kitchen, and straight into the washing machine. Three points for my basketball hero!

Married life was bliss—*for just about seven days!*

As I was doing the laundry every day, it began to dawn on me why the kitchen floor was always littered with hay. When I took Randy's socks out of the washer and unrolled them for the dryer, hay and other bits and pieces from the barnyard fell onto my clean kitchen floor. And I'd have to sweep it *again*!

After a couple of weeks, the ball of socks and hay routine started getting on my nerves, so I did what any sensible Southern woman would do.

After a really nice dinner of fried chicken, mashed potatoes, biscuits, and gravy, I served up a big bowl of homemade banana pudding. As Randy was digging in, I began, "Dumpling, before you show me your basketball trick again, it'd be nice if you'd shake the hay out of your socks on the porch."

What I was hoping he would say was, "Of course, Baby Doll."

But what he said was, "Hmm, hmm. Sure. Pass some more banana pudding over here."

As you might have guessed, that approach didn't work at all. The next day he was back shooting washing machine baskets with his hay-filled socks! So I did the only other thing I could think of. I began to nag just a little bit. This was a side of me that Randy had not seen before, so I thought it might be effective.

When he got home the next day, I was ready! I listened for the truck, positioned myself in the foyer and waited while he took off his boots. And just about the time he was puckering up for a kiss, I said, "If you think for one minute that I'm going to wash your clothes, iron your shirts, cook your meals, meet you at the door with a kiss, AND sweep up the hay from YOUR dirty socks, you have another think coming!"

Randy just kind of stood there, looking at me. And then he began to speak very slowly and very quietly. He gently reminded me that he had been a bachelor before, and he could be a bachelor again. "It won't take much to turn this romance cottage back into a bachelor pad," he declared.

So for the next few days, I washed his clothes. I ironed his shirts. I cooked his meals. But I did not meet him at the door with a kiss!

My visions of a romantic cottage were quickly melting before my eyes. I was becoming sadder and sadder. I knew this was no way to live. I had to let go of this irritation somehow.

Then, out of nowhere, I hit on the solution.

I washed his socks—ball and all. But when I took them out of the washer, instead of separating them, I left them in a ball. I then took the ball of socks out of the dryer and put them in Randy's drawer. In a ball!

Do you know that you can dry a ball of socks for twenty-four hours and they will still be damp on the inside? Not to mention still full of dirt and hay! Whose problem was it now?

I think Randy got the message, and I think I learned a lesson. I was letting a little dirt and hay knock me off balance. If I was going to experience my vision of Randy and me growing old together, a little compromising had to be done, priorities put in order, and Southern dinners cooked (served with a big bowl of homemade banana pudding)!

After sixteen years of marriage, I still meet Randy at the door with a kiss. The honeymoon cabin has evolved into a family lodge. The washing machine and dryer are in a new laundry room—out of site and out of range for shooting *hoops*. Randy has retired from farming and become a tennis hero of sorts, so now his socks are usually full of clay from the tennis court.

And Randy does the laundry—part of the time anyway!

The Distance From Fame
to Shame is Short!

I hung up the phone and did a little victory dance in the office. It was 1998 and I had been a professional speaker for about five years. My keynote presentations had been heard all over the mid-west and most of the Southern states, except Georgia. Now, finally, I was going to be a star in my own backyard. A major Atlanta hospital asked me to be the opening keynote speaker at a women's conference. When I heard that Lauren Hutton was going to be the closing keynoter, I was even more excited. *The* Lauren Hutton—a super model from the '60s, '70s and into the '90s!

Lauren and me! Both keynote speakers at the same conference. Lauren and Me! Both our photos in the same brochure as *featured* speakers. Lauren and Me! Probably close girlfriends before the event was over. I was impressed with myself!

A few days before the event, I got another call. My client had arranged for Lauren to appear as a guest on a morning television talk show the day before the women's conference. For whatever reason, Lauren was not going to be available and I was asked to take her place. Another victory dance!

I couldn't wait! I'd show the viewers who the real star was. Why, I would be so good during my five-minute segment that the television audience would demand to see me again for at least thirty minutes. After that, some high-level television executive would see me and recognize my star power and insist that I host my own talk-show program. Move over Oprah, Rosie, and Dr. Laura . . . Dr. Shirl was a celebrity-in-waiting!

Immediately after getting the call, I headed to my favorite shop to pick out the perfect outfit. I chose a two-piece suit in an exquisite shade of blue—and the style was "Oh, so cool!" When I took the suit by Mama's apartment for an opinion, she thought it was much too short. What did she know about fashion trends and television debuts?

I arrived at the station calm and collected on the outside, electrified with energy and anticipation on the inside. I was escorted to the studio to wait my turn for the pre-show meeting with the hostess. It wasn't as glamorous as I expected. She briefly explained that I was scheduled to be the last guest on the program that day. Then she told me the question she planned to ask me on the air, giving me sufficient time to prepare my answer. She probably thought I was a novice, but after only a couple of minutes together, she quickly left to connect with her other guests. She realized they needed more preparation than I did. She knew star quality when she saw it.

Looking around at the other guests appearing on the show, I figured out why the hostess had saved me until last. Everything would build to the finale. Just before the program aired, the chef was in the studio kitchen preparing a gourmet seafood entrée to share with the television audience. About the time he finished cooking, the cat from the Humane Society (another featured guest) escaped and followed his nose to the fish! Pandemonium broke out as people chased, caught, and caged the cat. As I was not involved in the debacle, I was feeling exceptionally cool and collected watching the chaos.

Next up was a group of female ethnic, dancers / drummers. They sashayed, they wiggled, and they beat their drums into a frenzy! I supposed the reason they were wearing only the slightest clothing was that garments would have interfered with their arm bracelets, toe rings, hair ornaments, and pylon-length fingernails!

After one more act, a beauty makeover complete with *Trailer Trash Pink* nail polish, it was my turn. Only seconds until I would be in front of the camera. The director, or maybe it was the assistant director, led me to the set and told me to sit on the sofa. The sofa was deep, lush, and plush. I sank into it, my knees practically flying up in front of me! Quickly, before the commercial ended and the program resumed, I adjusted my skirt, which all of a sudden seemed entirely too short. I *perched* on the edge of the sofa, became familiar with the cameras, moistened my lips, and smiled.

The hostess calmly took her position, sipped coffee, and reviewed her notes. As the director called, "Action!," I discreetly covered my knees with both hands, crossed my legs at the ankle, and sat forward. The hostess made very brief introductory remarks and then turned to me with a question. Not the question I was prepared to brilliantly answer. A different question! In fact, after a pause of several seconds, I looked at her and burst out with, "I don't know!" I followed my confession with a horsy, nervous laugh! Recovering quickly, I came up with another answer as the hostess focused on my co-guest, the vice president of the hospital that had hired me for the women's event.

Finally the interview was over. My moments of fame were over! My moments of shame were rapidly sinking in. I swallowed the lump in my throat, freshened my lipstick, and took a tour of the station, including a stop by the CEO's office for a brief chat. I discovered he was the brother of the vice president of the hospital, my client, the person who had just rescued me. Thank goodness he was gracious and did not mention my disastrous television debut.

As I got into the car to drive home, a few tears plopped onto my new blue jacket, and I fought to regain composure. All I could think about was that thousands of people had seen me make a fool of myself, but I tried to find some redeeming value about the morning's experience.

Finally, I did. I thought: I won't have to get up at the crack of dawn every day to host a television program; a younger, slimmer, and shorter friend will love my new outfit; and the trailer trash pink nail polish will really look great with my summer sandals!

But I still dreaded going home to face the music. When I got home, Mama called to tell me that she thought I did a great job! No mention of the short skirt. Randy, who had been watching, asked me why I sat with my hands crossed over my knees. Neither pointed out my less than stellar performance. The good news was that no one else I knew even saw the program! Too bad, they would have loved the drummers.

The next day, I did what I normally do. I presented an inspiring and humorous keynote and received a standing ovation from hundreds of women. But just as I was feeling a bit too full of myself, I remembered the previous morning at the television studio. Suddenly, I was a little more humbled and a little more appreciative of the applause and attention. I remembered that the distance between fame and shame is a very short one indeed.

He's a Good Egg

My Daddy's name was Aubrie B. Duncan. The *B* didn't stand for anything, but in Carroll County, Georgia, a child had to be given a middle name. That must be a Southern thing, so your mama can use your middle name just to make sure you know you are in serious trouble—as in, "Shirley *Ann*, you better get in here right now!"

Anyway, Daddy's family must have run out of middle names, so they simply chose the letter B for his. It balanced with the name of his twin sister, Audie Belle Duncan.

Maybe Aubrie seemed a bit pretentious for a baby, so their family always called him "Boy" and Aunt Audie, "Girl." After he left home to go the University of Georgia, he became known as Duncan. And eventually, he was affectionately known as "Dunc" by Mama and their close friends.

Thus Daddy became known as *Unc Dunc* to his many nieces and nephews—or, on giggling occasions, *Uncle Duncle!*

Daddy was a morning person. He got up early, made the coffee, read the local paper, and then began fixing breakfast for the family. He was always the breakfast cook at home, except some Saturdays when we all slept late and Mama fixed pancakes.

Mama just couldn't seem to get going in the mornings, but she could stay up all night grading papers, talking, or playing cards. Daddy said he learned early on in the marriage that if he was going to have a pleasant morning, he would cook, awaken Mama with coffee, and have breakfast on the table.

When the kids came along, it just seemed natural to let us sleep as late as possible, and awaken to the aroma of breakfast cooking in the kitchen.

We occasionally had cereal or cream of wheat or cheese toast. But our regular and favorite breakfast was bacon, toast with jelly, and scrambled eggs. Daddy made the best scrambled eggs in the whole wide world. They were light and fluffy, warm and moist.

On weekdays, after our breakfast, Daddy would put on his suit and tie and head out the door to open up the school for the day. Mary and I would do the dishes (giving Mama a little more quiet time). Then "the girls," as Daddy called us, spent the rest of the early morning rushing to get ready for school.

As Mary and I became older and the morning dressing ritual required more attention, Daddy would awaken us *while* he was cooking breakfast so we could get a head start on hair and makeup. And, bless his heart, he would even plug in our Lady Clairol electric rollers so they would be heated up when we got out of bed. What a guy!

Daddy's morning ritual continued after he retired. Mama still had a couple more years to teach, so he just resumed his coffee, paper, and breakfast routine. This time dressed in khaki pants and faded shirts instead of that suit and tie.

Then life took a bad turn. Daddy had a stroke and was very, very sick. As he got better, the first thing he wanted to do was cook breakfast for Mama. One of my most heart breaking memories is walking into the kitchen and finding him throwing away burnt toast. The bacon grease was hot and smoking, and the uncooked eggs were spilled all over the kitchen counter. I stuck around to help him clean up and to start over. This time, I watched the bacon and toast, leaving the eggs to him. Thank God they turned out perfectly. Thank God Daddy had not been robbed of everything.

Several years later, I was fixing breakfast for Cousin Martha Jean and some more company we had. As she took her first bite of eggs, she exclaimed, "Oh, Unc Dunc eggs! I haven't had these in years." At that moment, I realized I had learned, inherited, or stumbled on a family treasure: cooking perfect scrambled eggs.

Like Daddy, I like to get up a little early, enjoy the solitude of the morning, and greet Randy with a cup of coffee, the local newspaper, and breakfast. And when we have company, there's nothing I enjoy more than cooking bacon, toast with jelly, and Unc Dunc eggs.

Of course, I'm almost guaranteed someone will exclaim, "These are the best eggs I've ever eaten! How do you make them?" I tell the story and then describe how it's done.

Unc Dunc eggs have become the most requested food for returning family and guests. People ask for the recipe and the secret ingredient.

So here it is for you. It's a simple recipe. The ingredients are eggs. Regular "ole" store-bought eggs. The skill is in the preparation.

> Place cracked eggs into a mixing bowl (generally one—two per person served).
>
> Using a whisk or an eggbeater, beat eggs until fluffy. Not

just a little bit fluffy, but really fluffy.

Use butter, margarine, or cooking spray to lightly coat the skillet.

Put the skillet on a stove unit heated to medium high.

Give the eggs one last whisk and slowly pour them into the skillet.

Let the eggs begin to cook and *gently* fold/stir the eggs.

Remove from heat just before the eggs finish cooking (there should be no liquid egg left—just soft, fluffy eggs). They will finish cooking as they are being served.

Serve.

As simple as the recipe is, people inevitably phone me for clarification. They just can't seem to get the eggs to come out exactly right. They want to add milk or cream or more butter. I always have to explain that it's not the ingredients, it is the process.

It's about intention, timing, and focus.

When Daddy cooked our breakfast, *he did it out of love* (and perhaps a little self-preservation). He took the time to really beat the eggs (using an old-fashioned crank beater). He didn't just give them a *lick and a promise*; he took the time to do it right.

And he paid close attention to the temperature of the skillet, letting it get warm, but not too hot. He watched over the eggs while they cooked, making sure that he gently folded them. Then he would watch the consistency to take them off at just the perfect time.

In repeating the instructions many times, I have finally learned the other secret to Unc Dunc eggs. The secret is in the joy of the work. The secret is in knowing that a simple task can bring a morning smile to the faces of family and friends. The secret is about staying in the present. And most of all, the secret is about making Unc Dunc eggs with love.

PS: A little grated sharp cheddar cheese in the eggs makes 'em even better!

The Courage Muscle

I have a fear. It's kind of a secret, because I know that if people find out about it they will use it against me, they will torment me with it. And they will always be on the lookout for my vulnerability. And just when I don't expect it, they will ZAP me.

But every once in a while, life will throw you the ZAP—just to test your courage muscle.

Here's how it happened to me.

During the summer of 2000, I was at the annual convention of the National Speakers Association in San Antonio, Texas. I was the newly elected president of the Georgia chapter and was rushing around the convention with the added responsibilities of chapter leadership. One day, the temperature was 103 degrees outside, and about 100 degrees inside. That afternoon, I found myself huddled inside an elevator so packed that I was afraid the man behind me was thinking I might be getting *fresh!*

The express elevator bypassed the first twenty-four floors and quickly soared to the first stop. The doors opened on the 25th floor and a couple got off—and wouldn't you know, three more people squeezed in. As the doors closed, the man behind me shifted uncomfortably as we became even more intimate.

Like most elevator rides, all the passengers had their heads tilted slightly upward waiting for the lights to blink for the 26th floor—where a lot us were getting off. We all gasped when all the lights started blinking sporadically—like running lights on a Christmas tree! Then, with no warning, the elevator started to go down.

Because it was designed to bypass floors one through twenty-four, there were no lights signaling those floors. We had no concept of space and distance . . . it felt like a free fall!

This is where thinking and blood pressure accelerate to record levels. I began talking to myself: "If I jump up, will I be hurt when I land? If I jump up *just* before impact, will I land on everybody else, softening the blow? Will Randy miss me if this is my Waterloo? Will everybody be as sad as I hope they will be if this is a fatality?" And, "Who will take care of Mama?"

After the longest ten seconds in the world's history, we landed gently and normally on the ground floor. As the doors opened, my usually good manners flew right out the window. I literally jumped over three layers of people to be the first one out of the elevator. Standing outside, I felt my breathing resume and realized my heart was actually still inside my chest.

Composing myself, I turned to smile at my traveling companions. A few had stepped off and away from the elevator. One courteous passenger was holding the door and the rest were waiting to see if I wanted to take a second ride up that long elevator shaft.

My first reaction was, "Are you crazy? Do you not realize that we could have all just died? Don't you know that I'm not sure that everybody will miss me as much as I want them to? Do you not realize that there is probably a woman out there somewhere just waiting for something like this to happen so she can move into my house? The very house I have just completely remodeled to suit Randy and me until we are at least a hundred? And whoever this brazen woman is, do you think she is going to look after *my* mama?"

The people waiting to close the doors and start the ride back to the 26th floor just didn't *get it*.

Then I started to *get it*, as I thought about my alternatives. The stairwell leading to the 26th floor was not air-conditioned. I had on rather sassy, but uncomfortable, high-heeled shoes. I had on a suit that so far was good for another wear before dry cleaning. But my biggest concern was that I was scheduled to lead a very important meeting in only twenty minutes in the hotel next door. And the materials I needed were on the 26th floor!

Snap decisions are tough things to make.

Besides, in that split-second, the basis of my fear reached up and grabbed me. I realized that my fear was not from the fact that the elevator might crash—I had a game plan for that. The absolutely terrorizing, paralyzing fear was the fact that I thought the door might not open. Somewhere in the deep recesses of my memory, I recalled a sadness of my very early life.

Memories flooded my brain. Memories not about an elevator. Memories of a basement room. Memories of a birth mother who did not understand discipline and used *locking up* as punishment. Memories of a terrifying fear that the door would never open again and I would never again experience light and sunshine. Fear that I would be forgotten and left behind in a move. Memories of my greatest fear—that I was locked up for good.

I remembered how hard my wonderful adopted parents

tried to ease those fears. They never required me to shut the bathroom door when I was little. A light was left on all night in my room—even when I was a teenager. I was never forced to ride an elevator. I was never shamed or teased when I climbed the steps to get to an appointment.

These were memories that had been locked away for years—and ZAP! in a split second, life had made me three years old again.

Standing there—outside the elevator with ten people waiting expectantly—I had a decision to make. Looking at the track on the floor where the doors opened and closed, I knew I could step over the metal line and address the fear head on—or I could smile sweetly and walk away. No one would know the battle I was fighting.

I stepped over the line. I turned and watched the doors close.

My heart was still wildly beating. My palms were a little damp. And the jury was still out on whether or not the suit would be good for another wearing. More importantly, I retrieved my materials, changed my clothes, exchanged my heels for sassy walking shoes, and headed to the meeting.

In the meeting, I found renewed strength in my ability to lead: to address rather delicate and uncomfortable issues and to clarify tactfully, yet firmly, a sticky situation with some of the *good ole boys*. I found the courage to lead.

In my pre-elevator-scare life, I would have hemmed and hawed and tried to figure out a way to make it all work without hurting anybody's feelings. After all, I was new at this leadership role and didn't want to create friction at my first official meeting.

But I'd stepped over the line just a few minutes before. I'd crossed a bigger hurdle than the issue in this room. My courage muscle had had a workout and become stronger. I'd become braver.

With composure I did not know I owned, I took a deep breath and became a leader.

Fear is paralyzing—fear is immobilizing—fear keeps me stuck. Letting go of fear takes a lot of courage. But when I do, something else happens. Every time I exercise my courage muscle, I move to a higher level of confidence. I like that.

State of Reunion

It comes in the mail every winter. The reminder that the Duncan family reunion will be held in July. If Mama were alive, she would be distressed about what food to prepare. I don't know why she worried. I've been fixing the food for our family since we began this new generation of reunions. I think she just liked to give me a gentle reminder to plan ahead of time, something I don't always do.

Getting the notice and planning the food reminded me that Duncan reunions have changed in many ways over the past thirty or so years.

When I was growing up, the most exciting part of summer (other than our beach vacation) was going to the Duncan family reunion. We went to Uncle Amon's farm, just outside of Athens, Georgia. Back then, we always got together during the hot, sweltering days of August. It seemed that we rode for hours with the car windows down. When we finally passed by the University of Georgia, we knew we would get to the farm within minutes. Mary and I always had a contest to see who could spot the first sign of the pasture—the signal that we were finally there!

As we turned in the opening and crossed the cattle gap into the freshly bush-hogged pasture, I'd be sitting on the edge of the seat. I couldn't wait to see who was at the fishing pond, to see if anybody was already playing baseball (cow patties for bases), to see if horseshoes and croquet had started, and most of all, to see which of my older cousins had already arrived.

When we crossed the second cattle gap, we were in the cool shaded yard of the cabin. Mary and I opened the car doors before Daddy had a chance to get completely stopped. And after suffering a brief moment of sudden shyness, we would begin unloading. (I've always found that having a task to do helps ease me into the first awkward moments at most social events). First, Daddy carried a fat, ripe watermelon to the spring so it would be icy cold at cutting time. It took several more trips to carry the bags of groceries and boxes of food to the eating porch and kitchen. Suitcases and overnight bags had to be dropped off in the sleeping areas. As we grew into teenagers, Mary and I added make-up cases to our luggage sets—a signature item among girls who wanted to proclaim their womanhood.

Walking up the stairs into the cabin was a heady experience. The long eating porch and small, adjacent kitchen took up the entire length of one side of the cabin. The plywood window covers were open and hooked at the ceiling to allow the summer breeze to flow through the upstairs. A long table/counter below the window created the feeling of being out-of-doors, but the screen provided protection from the nightly *skeeter* invasion.

Aunt Florice and Aunt Mae and Aunt Alera would be in the kitchen organizing the food for the weekend. Enough tomatoes, cucumbers, and cantaloupes to feed an army were peeled and sliced. Fresh corn had to be shucked, peas shelled, and okra cut up for frying. Gallons upon gallons of very sweet iced tea were readied to quench the summer thirsts, and somewhere, hidden away, was Aunt Florice's homemade coconut cake. (The Duncans always had a sweet tooth—they even sprinkled sugar on their tomatoes!)

Aunt Audie was either in the kitchen seeing that everything was in order for her biscuit-making—or in the "big room" reading *Reader's Digest Condensed Books* with Aunt Bernice. Aunt Bernice was never one to offer too much kitchen help. She was single and lived in Atlanta in an apartment and worked as an administrative assistant. She had a very important job working for a very important man. But during family reunion time, Aunt Bernice was on vacation!

Mama, Aunt Bea, and Aunt Mildred would be helping out any way the others needed them to.

Nearby, on one of the many daybeds, Aunt Mickey, the baby sister of the Duncan family, was usually reclining. She would be recovering from a headache, operation, or other recently incurred maladies. She was always a little frail, unlike her strong siblings.

The big room consisted of a great stone fireplace—daybeds, reading lamps and chairs along every wall. In the middle of the room were card tables and five or six conversation areas. At the far end of the great room, there was a paneled room just big enough for a double bed, and a bathroom just big enough for one person and her make-up case.

Across from the bathroom, concrete steps led down to the "dorm rooms." Each room held bunk beds and daybeds. There was enough room to sleep all the cousins and a chaperoning aunt. It took several years before I was brave enough to sleep in the basement. But once I reached a certain age, the back room of the basement was the ideal place for my just-older cousin,

Sylvia, to tell me all about the secrets of dating and boyfriends.

After "oohs" and "ahs" and "My, how much you've grown," and "Aren't you turning into a young lady, now!" and "Are you making all As in school?" and on and on and on, we'd get down to the real family reunion. I could never decide where to begin. I loved playing badminton, volleyball, and croquet, and, as my adolescence took over, I loved quiet walks down by the creek.

Everybody had fun at the family reunion on the farm. Daddy and the uncles would barbecue chickens over the large, specially designed outdoor pit. Uncle Amon taught agriculture education at the University of Georgia and kept up with the latest trends. He talked of cattle and crops with his brothers and they listened closely. They had all grown up chopping cotton and grinding meal, and none of them ever got very far away from their farming roots.

The Duncan boys were quite competitive, whether it was croquet, horseshoes, golf, Rook or, as Mama used to say, "Just a game of tiddlywinks." But there were certain things they agreed on: the Georgia Bulldogs were the best team in the country and being a family man was the most important job a person could have.

I loved watching those brothers and brothers-in-law share golf stories, debate political issues, and most of all, laugh their horsy, mouth-wide-open Duncan laugh. As I watched, my heart was so full, but I didn't understand why at the time. That understanding would come later.

We ate watermelon, we fished (and seldom caught anything), and we went on hayrides. We caught lightning bugs, played hide-and-go-seek at dusk, and sat outside whispering until the grown-ups called us in. We played scrabble and cards, we read, and we ate. And ate, and ate, and ate. We had pancakes and eggs and fruit for breakfast; tomato sandwiches and chips for lunch; barbecued chicken and all the vegetables our aunts had spent days preparing for dinner.

Aunt Alera would bring the latest craft fad for us all to try. She was a Home Demonstration Agent and worked with the 4-H Clubs. One year, we made jewelry out of safety pins and beads. Another year, we heated marbles in the oven then dropped them into cold water. The inside of the marbles cracked, creating a special crystal effect that made pretty necklaces and ear bobs.

I spent a lot of time daydreaming at Uncle Amon's. Maybe my fantasies came from watching the older boy cousins, whom I rarely got to see. Or maybe they came from my older female cousins who were attending the University of Georgia. I was in awe of their poise and self-assuredness.

My cousins talked about something called *rush*, and then one summer they were getting *pinned*, and eventually magnificent weddings were planned. The girl cousins were so pretty and they had handsome boyfriends, soon-to-be husbands. I looked at them wistfully, vowing that one day I, too, would have such a storybook life.

But the boy cousins were more my speed. They laughed and teased, and cut up with Mary and me. They included us in their activities—until they, too, started getting ready for college. Once again, I found myself on the outside, wistfully dreaming that time would either hurry and catch me up or slow me down—and not let my life get any more complicated or confusing than it already was.

I was very awkward, clumsy, and unkempt at thirteen and the male cousins had outgrown me. I felt caught in the middle—like a spirited child, but wanting to be a sophisticated teenager.

As if it were yesterday, I remember one summer's eve sitting on the bumper of a convertible that belonged to a really cool cousin. Another cousin had stopped by the car, looked at me sideways, and said, "Shirley, you are going to be a very beautiful girl someday!" I remember that I blushed, I giggled, and suddenly my spirit filled with magnificent hope of days to come. It was the first time in my life I had heard these words (from someone other than a parent). It was the best gift I could have received that summer and a memory that makes me smile to this day.

Many years have passed since that last Duncan reunion at Uncle Amon's farm. Now we get together in other places—usually just for the day. Cousin Tim shares his updated research about the Duncan family tree. He traveled all the way to Scotland just to get in touch with some of our family roots.

Me? I want to step back, just one more warm summer evening, to that cabin outside of Athens, Georgia, and listen once again to the horsy, wide-open-mouth Duncan laugh.

That's where my roots are and my heart is.

Saving Grace

When I was thirteen, going on fourteen, my Gillham cousins (on Mama's side of the family) asked me to go to church camp with them. We lived in the country and attended a small rural church that had just a handful of young people. The cousins lived in Atlanta and attended a huge church with a lot of young people. In fact, it was large enough to have a youth program *and* a large youth choir.

The camp we were going to was Ridgecrest Baptist Assembly, nestled in the Smoky Mountains of North Carolina, just outside of Asheville. The camp was 300 miles away from home—300 miles away from my parents—a coed camp—and the icing on the cake, it was music week. I couldn't wait to go!

And just like I do today when I have something exciting going on, I lie in bed at night and envision what will take place. Because the camp was Southern Baptist, I knew there would be a revival every night—and I had heard that the biggest revival would be on Friday night for everyone who had not yet been "saved."

I pictured myself at that last camp revival meeting. I would be standing behind the pulpit, in the spotlight, singing a solo. It would be *Amazing Grace* and, as the song ended, all the campers would jump to their feet and give me a standing ovation. The best part of the dream was that my yet-to-be-named camp boyfriend would be waiting for me to step down from the platform. And as he reached for my hand, he would whisper in my ear, "Let's walk through the prayer garden just one more time."

Have you ever had dreams that did not come true? That did not come out just the way you imagined them?

What really happened at camp was this: On the first day, we were put into small groups of eighteen to twenty people. Knowing that the choir director in charge of each group would be picking out the solo voices, I was ready. Our group began to sing an old hymn, *The Old Rugged Cross*. But, before we even got through the words, "On a hill far-away," the choir director stopped us and in a booming voice, he said, "Someone is off-key!"

His words didn't bother me. I didn't know what a key was! We started and were stopped again. Same remark, same non-response. Finally, after several attempts at starting and stopping, I decided to help out the choir director. After all, if we didn't move ahead, we would never get to my solo part.

While the rest of our choir sang, I simply mouthed the words, listening carefully to discover who was off key. I didn't hear anything unusual—and evidently the choir director didn't either. He started smiling and continued to direct us, beaming as we finished. "That was perfect!" he exclaimed.

I knew three things at the end of that song. Number one, I could not sing. Number two, everybody else already knew I could not sing. And number three, and probably the most tragic of all, there would be no walking through the prayer garden on Friday night after my thunderous ovation.

However, I was not going to be discouraged. I've always looked at situations like these with a fresh perspective, and tended to make the best of most situations. I decided right then and there that it would be simpler to go through life just lip-synching. I have discovered that lots of people do the same thing. It isn't hard to learn to do, and it lets me enjoy pretending to sing without offending anyone. I've noticed that choir directors appreciate it.

I didn't think much about the decision to lip-sync until I was much older and life had taken a lot of twists and turns.

When I was twenty-four years old, Daddy had a stroke. He was so sick that by the time I arrived at the hospital that he wasn't expected to live. In fact, the doctor was so sure that Daddy would not recover that he suggested Mama prepare herself and the rest of the family for his impending death.

I found Mama in the Intensive Care Unit waiting room sitting in a dimly lit corner. She was surrounded by friends and family. She had a steno pad on her lap and a pencil in her hand. I moved closer to see what she was doing. She was doing exactly what the doctor had suggested. She was planning Daddy's funeral.

Mama had decided on the pallbearers—all old friends of Daddy's. Our minister would "preach" Daddy's funeral sermon. And, of course, Lamar's wife, Judy, would sing *Amazing Grace*. It was Daddy's favorite hymn and Judy had a professionally trained voice. She had been entertaining our family for years with her gift of song.

The wonder of it all is that Daddy didn't die. In fact, he lived for many more years. The final years were difficult. There were lots of down hills in his health, and very few up hills. We were often called to the hospital to come quickly, never knowing if this would be the end.

About seven years ago, I rushed to the hospital to join Mama in Daddy's room. No more heroics—no more ICUs. Daddy was quietly resting and Mama was in the corner with the steno pad in her lap. She was still working on Daddy's funeral. There were some glitches, though. The original pallbearers had already died! The minister was retired and not in good enough health to "preach" the funeral. And Lamar was no longer married to the singing sister-in-law!

But Mama had everything figured out. She had already chosen new pallbearers and one of her favorite young preachers would conduct the service. However, she was anxious to talk with me about the music.

She said, "Shirley Ann, I want to talk with you about something, but I don't want to hurt your feelings." (I always get nervous when people say things like that to me.) She quickly told me that she had decided that the children, the grandchildren, and the nieces and nephews would sing *Amazing Grace* at Daddy's funeral. Then she turned to me and said, "Baby Doll, if you'd like to, you can stand up there with them and mouth the words!"

I looked very gently into Mama's eyes and quietly replied, "Mama, I won't mouth the words to anything."

Surprised, she answered, "Oh?"

"No ma'am, " I repeated, "I won't mouth the words to anything!"

With that, I walked over to my Daddy's bedside table, picked up a cup, and took a sip of water. Then I lifted his hand and placed it in mine. I thought about what a fine man he was.

What a wonderful school man he was, who had given so much of himself to the rural communities where he had served. And what a wonderful daddy—the man who had adopted two little girls, sight unseen, and always gave us a loving home.

Then I turned to Mama with love, and I thought about how unfailingly loyal she had been through these last hard years of Daddy's illness. I thought about how many children she too had inspired during her many years as a guidance counselor and teacher. I thought about the unfulfilled dreams of retirement she had selflessly abandoned. And in that moment, I loved my mama more than ever.

And then I straightened my shoulders, lifted my head, and stood in that hospital room and sang *Amazing Grace!*

To them, I sang an *amazing Amazing Grace*. In tune, on key, and acappella!

How did I recapture my childhood joy of singing? From my grandchildren!

Remembering how much I loved to sing in the car with Mama and Daddy, I sang to my grandchildren as we rode together in the car. We sang all sorts of fun songs with funny words and even funnier expressions. We sang *Do Your Ears Hang Low?*, *Five Little Monkeys Swinging in the Tree*, and we always ended with *Jesus Loves The Little Children*. And just as we finished a song, they would look over and say, "One more time, Gran-Gran. One more time." They never once mentioned off key!

After so much singing in the car with them, I realized that I had learned to sing. Maybe not perfectly all the time, but perfect enough for bringing the joy of music back into my life.

A few months later, Daddy died. At his funeral, I did what I do best. I delivered the eulogy on behalf of our family, and when my part was over, I stepped off the pulpit and joined my siblings and other family members to sing *Amazing Grace* with them.

Sometimes I sang alto with Cousin Martha Jean. Sometimes I sang soprano with my niece Valerie. Sometimes I sang tenor with my brother Lamar. And every once in a while, I sang bass with Cousin Butch. The important thing is not *how* I sang, but *that* I sang.

It takes a parent to bring out the music in our hearts, and sometimes it takes a child to remind us what really matters. And that, my friends, is saving grace.

Joseph Was a Step Daddy

During the weeks before Christmas 1993, I was arranging one of several nativities with the assistance of one of my grandsons, Zeke. He particularly liked to organize the figures, telling me the role each one played in the Christmas story.

Since it was still several days before Christmas, he put the three Wise Men on the far end of the table and the manger scene on the other end (the Wise Men would steadily move closer to the Baby Jesus each day during Advent). Placing Mary next to Baby Jesus, he said, "This is Jesus's mama, Mary." Then he picked up the Joseph figure and said, "This is God."

Immediately I corrected him and explained that the figure was of Joseph, not God. "But I thought God *was* Jesus's daddy" he replied. "Isn't Jesus God's son?"

Boy, was I ever stumped! I stammered, looking for the right words to describe the situation, and then gave a lame explanation that God was in Heaven and that Mary was married to Joseph on earth—and I kept looking for the right answer.

Suddenly Zeke's eyes lit up as he said, "I get it. Joseph was a *step*-daddy."

At the moment, I thought, "Well, no, not really." And then I realized what a great answer I had just been given. Later, reflecting on the moment, I was overwhelmed with the image that Joseph was a step-daddy—maybe the very first step-daddy.

As I thought more and more about it, I realized that God provided Jesus with someone to serve as His earthly father—to be a constant physical presence in His life. Joseph did the day-to-day parenting: teaching Jesus how to fish, showing Him how to build things, and taking Him to the synagogue. Yet, God didn't give up his parental rights. He never ceased to be in contact and communication with His son.

Thinking it all through, I realized that Zeke understood that Joseph was a stepdaddy because he had one of his own. Steve, married to Cindy (Zeke's mother), was his day-to-day dad. Teaching him to play ball, taking him camping, and helping with his homework. And Steve never tried to deny Scott, Zeke's *real* dad, the opportunity to be with his son. Zeke understood this at a fundamental level.

And then rather sheepishly, I remembered that I was a step-mother . . . and a step-grandmother. I have no children of my very own, only those on loan to me from other mothers and grandmothers.

Suddenly, I was filled with pride as I felt a kinship with Joseph. God had given me the special privilege of caring for and influencing His children while honoring their *real* parents and grandparents. I like that.

I'm a Tap-Water Girl

in a Bottled-Water World

One hot summer day in 1998, I was driving to a tennis match when I realized I had forgotten my water jug. Since the weather was predicted to reach almost 100 degrees by noon and the humidity was about 85 percent, I pulled into a quick-market to get some water. Much to my surprise, I realized, that almost overnight, bottled water had become a marketing phenomenon! I couldn't believe how many options there were. Pint-size, half-liter, liter, squirt-top, twist-top, everything but a pop-top. Sparkling water, flavored water, plain water. All claiming to be from some pure mountain spring in the USA, Canada, or even Europe. I couldn't figure out which one to buy, so I bought a gallon jug of the cheapest brand. Back on the road with my valuable purchase, I recalled another incident with bottled water.

I was staying at an exclusive hotel in downtown Chicago. My client had arranged a room for me on the floor that included access to the elegant concierge lounge. Guests could enjoy an abundance of pastries and hors d'oeuvres, along with every imaginable kind of drink. The hostess on duty asked what I would like to drink and I replied, "I'll just have water." She immediately began apologizing that they were out of bottled water. I assured her that a glass of regular tap water would be just fine.

I immediately sensed that her impression of me dropped several notches. In fact, I suspect that she realized that I am not a frequent member of the concierge class—the *business elite* as they are known in the airline industry. During the rest of my visit, I knew there was no point putting on airs. I'd already become way too middle-class for this hostess.

Remembering that exchange made me laugh out loud in the car. And then I got even more tickled. I thought, "I have just paid $1.95 for a gallon of water. When taxes were added, it was over $2.00! I realized I had just paid more for my water than for a soft drink! In fact, I could have bought a gallon of gasoline for less than I paid for the water!"

And that got me to thinking: When did bottled water become so fashionable? Where had I been? Bottled water has become something of a status symbol. It seems that everywhere I turned, people are walking up and down the street sipping bottled water and talking on their cell phones. On airplanes, flight attendants pass out more bottled water than any other beverage. And lately, when I go into an executive's office, it isn't unusual to see bottles of water on the credenza. I have friends who have bottled water delivered to their kitchen on a regular basis. I always feel like I'm in a waiting room somewhere when I flip the handle and watch the water in the jug take a big gulp of air as I fill my glass. As a kid, it was always a treat to get water out of one of those big blue gulping jugs.

When I was a kid, I would have never imagined that I would

someday buy water in bottles at the convenience store. I just went to the refrigerator and got water out of the water pitcher. And if I got the last of the water, I knew to refill the pitcher from the kitchen tap.

At Uncle Amon's farm, we got water out of the spring—just above the spot where the watermelons were cooling. Once my sister, Mary, got sick with a rash, and we filled water bottles for her from the deep, dark, intriguing well at Aunt Audie's house. On hot Georgia summer days, we'd stop our play just long enough to get a drink out of the garden hose; we always had to remember to let the water run for a minute so it wouldn't be too warm or taste like rubber! During my backpacking days, I cupped my hands and dipped them into a cool mountain stream to quench my thirst (something I'm sternly warned against this day and time). At the cabin where I spent some of my young adult life, we primed the pump and got water out of the well (it was always a chore late at night, in the dead of winter). And when the pump went out or the power was down, we "toted" water from the stream. I also recall taking my older friend, Millie, to a waterfall on a weekly basis to fill her water jugs with fresh mountain water.

But most of all, I remember getting water straight from the tap. Most of the time, I'd grab one of our matching jelly glasses, fill it with water, gulp it down, slam the screen door, and be back outside playing kick-the-can before Mama could figure out who had come through the kitchen like a whirlwind. I rarely bothered putting ice in my water, since that meant emptying and then refilling the ice trays. That slowed me down too much.

Of course, at our house we also drank a whole lot of iced tea. The kind that had enough real sugar in it that only so much would dissolve and the rest would sink to the bottom of the glass. That last sip of tea was the coldest and sweetest taste in the world. Iced tea was for lunch and supper, and for sipping while sitting on porches on summer evenings.

Sometimes we could have a Coke too. No more than one a day. The real kind—in a bottle with a cap. The bottle opener was on the doorframe just inside the kitchen door, or tied to a string on a nail on the counter. Wherever it was, opening a bottle of ice-cold Coke was a treat, and one that didn't happen everyday at our house.

But the main beverage in my diet has always been water. The tap kind, not the bottled kind. And I reckon I have a little resistance to buying into the water fad. Perhaps it's just a little stubbornness on my part. Or maybe I'd rather spend my money on something more fun.

Or perhaps, given my history, I'm just a tap water girl in a bottled water world.

Starry, Starry Night

Thanksgiving is my favorite holiday of all. Unlike Christmas, it doesn't get tangled up with gifts, parties, and decorations. Thanksgiving is about family, traditions, food, and hope.

First we go north to visit with my side of the family at Cousin Martha Jean and Jimmy Smith's farm in Haralson County, Georgia. They are the sixth generation of Smiths to live on the land and the fourth to live in the farmhouse.

By the time we arrive, Jimmy has spent days smoking hams and turkeys and gathering the ingredients for cornbread dressing and candied yams. He has picked, washed, and cooked turnip greens, and thawed the creamed corn we put up last summer. Now he is waiting for me to help with the giblet gravy. More cousins arrive with even more food. Yeast rolls, vegetable casseroles, salads, deviled eggs, and desserts. Enough desserts to last through Christmas, New Year's Day, and Super Bowl Sunday!

Martha Jean has spent days making sure that Jimmy gets it all done.

When we're ready to eat, the men who aren't in the kitchen sampling the food are summoned from the TV football game. Children are called from the yard where they have been playing football, chasing the cat, or riding the golf cart. We hold hands as the blessing is asked.

After about an hour of eating, eating, and more eating, we divide into two groups. Those who are going to nap and those who are going to shoot. Skeet, that is.

The adventurous ones load up on the back of a couple of pickup trucks and head to the pasture for skeet shooting. The best part is watching everyone tease, cajole, and rag each other about not hitting the skeet. The first time I tried shooting, I hit three orange targets in a row. I decided right then and there not to press my luck. Sister Mary usually names her targets (after a particular ex- husband) and manages to hit it squarely every time.

Martha Jean is supposedly very good at skeet shooting. She has her own gun—one that won't hurt her shoulder—and Jimmy takes her out to practice a few times before Thanksgiving. I guess the person releasing the skeet messes her up every time. With her great big brown eyes opened wide, she drawls, "Why, Jimmy, I just don't know what is wrong with my shooting today," and demurely smiles at everyone.

Naturally there are male cousins waiting for the girls and kids to finish so they can show us how it's done. By the time the guys shoot, the girls are gathered around the trucks catching up on family gossip and keeping little children out of cow patties. We don't pay a whole lot of attention to how it's done.

After a while, Randy and I take our leave to visit his side of the family. We head south to Heard County to the Heard family reunion at the ancestral home of Cousin Dock and Janie Davis. It's been in their family six generations too.

The atmosphere is usually verging on *wild* by the time we arrive. The flatbed trailer is filled with hay and hooked to the tractor. Parents are scurrying around trying to locate missing children and match coats, hats, and mittens. The kids are usually found on the trampoline or chasing puppies or hiding from older cousins.

I always go on the hayride and Randy always volunteers to stay at the house to keep company with the parents of the youngest babies—or the elders who can't make the ride. I've never really been sure what goes on at the house when we're off on the ride, but Randy seems to think he gets the best end of the deal by staying behind.

How do you fit twenty cousins, ranging from age nine months to sixty-five years, on a hay wagon? On top of each other, of course. We seldom fall off since we are wedged in so tightly. The ride begins with an attempt at singing. The first song is usually *Old McDonald*, followed by *She'll Be Coming 'Round the Mountain*. *Bingo*, the kids' favorite, is followed by a couple of Christmas carols and *Jingle Bells*. Some of the forty-something group always tries to remember the words to the theme songs from the *Beverly Hillbillies* and *Gilligan's Island*. Those songs generally start off with a bang and end with humming.

By this point, most everybody is cramped enough to need a break—and usually Dock provides it by crossing the creek, going up a hill halfway, backing down, going again, and then suggesting we unload and push up the hill. After everyone is accounted for and positions are reestablished, we go by the *haunted house* where the older "little ones" relate to the younger "little ones" about the ghost that resides there.

Finally, just before family joys turn into family squabbles, we unload next to a HUGE bonfire Dock has prepared. He douses the wood with kerosene and strikes the match. Adults spend the next twenty minutes discouraging flaming sword fights, loading marshmallow sticks, and serving juice to the children. The adults serve their own juice, which is usually in the form of wine. After everyone has gotten in touch with the *pyromaniac within*, we settle down for the ghost stories . . . the highlight of the evening.

Three-year-olds with lisps tell of the "one ahmed man, looking for his mithing ahm." The seven-to-twelve-year-olds compete for the goriest tale. Finally, the adults begin an add-on tale that leaves everyone depleted of ghosts, goblins, and one-armed monsters. And then we have a thankful circle where each person shares what he or she has been thankful for over the last year. The campfire outing ends with everyone holding hands and singing, *Blessed Be The Tie That Binds*.

Back on the flatbed and back to the farmhouse. The trip home is usually a quiet one, adults reflecting on the gift of the day and children snuggling in the hay or on their mamas' laps, trying hard to remember that the stories were only pretend.

One Thanksgiving night, we were particularly quiet, enjoying the bright, starry sky. Zeke was snuggled into my lap staring off into the night. Suddenly he whispered to me, "Gran-Gran, I see God."

"Where?" I asked.

"Up there—by that star," he pointed. Knowing that this discussion wasn't meant for everyone's ears, I waited to ask more questions.

In the truck going home, I asked Zeke if he wanted to tell Granddaddy and me about seeing God. "What do you want to know?" he replied.

Being curious, I asked Zeke, "What does God look like?"

"Oh, he looked all right," Zeke said with a casual shrug of his shoulders (as if to say, "What did you expect?"). "But God was holding Papa D in his hands like this," he continued as he formed an cradle with both hands, "and Papa D was young and Papa D was well."

Papa D, my daddy, had died about six weeks earlier. He had been bed ridden for the entirety of Zeke's life. Zeke knew him only as a very sick man whom we visited and fed on Sundays. Zeke always loved to go see Papa D and crank up the head of his bed, or stand in a chair and write on Papa D's message board, or even help eat Papa D's food (it was pureed and Zeke loved it). Somehow, that particular Thanksgiving, Zeke and God must have known that I needed to know that Papa D was well again.

Each year, we all arrive at Thanksgiving in the country a little bit different—impacted by our personal and collective joys and sorrows. Each year, someone is not there, and each year, someone new attends.

Most of us are actually kin to each other. But we always have honorary *kissing cousins* for the day. Regardless of who shows up, after a few minutes of brief reminders and introductions, the traditions, enveloped in the love of family, seem to create a spirit that gives us nourishment and hope, sustaining us for the next 364 days.

Kind of like seeing God on a starry, starry night!

Getting Old is Hell

Aunt Gladys, Mama's older sister, used to say, "Getting old is hell." Her younger siblings would look askance, pretending a little shock at her use of such vulgarity. That is, until they began to feel some of the vestiges of "old age" themselves.

In November 1999, those same siblings gathered together with other family members to celebrate Mama's 80th birthday. More than once, I heard them quote Aunt Gladys, who had died several years before. That night, someone else was missing from the party—Mama. Oh, she was there, physically, at least. Sitting in her wheelchair, smiling a crooked smile as everyone wished her a happy day and a happy year. But she wasn't really there.

There are moments of truth for every caregiver. My mother's 80th birthday party was such a reality moment for me. I realized that Mama was not going to get better and that she would never get *back to normal*. I clearly realized that she could no longer carry on small talk about this, that, and the other. She would no longer share the oft-told stories of our youth, no longer instigate the laughter that left tears running down our cheeks, and no longer remember all the connections of who is kin to whom, who lived in what house, and who resided in which community. And most importantly, she would not be able to remember and share all the little closet skeletons that are part of every family's history.

Mama was the epicenter of family news. She kept up with all the relatives and was the first to telephone when there was news to be shared. In fact, we often teased, "You can telephone or you can tel-a-Winnie!"

That night she smiled with half-awareness as her baby brothers joked and teased her. She made a few appropriate inquiries of great nieces and nephews, and a few inappropriate remarks. That night, her new favorite phrase was, "Well, nobody told *me* about that." There was no use pointing out that she had been told several times.

My heart ached. I asked myself, "What can I do? What can anybody do while watching the slow deterioration of loved ones?"

Suddenly I wanted to find a list of "Ten Easy Steps To Adjust To Caring For Aging Parents." I especially needed help for the moments when I ran out of patience. Suddenly I realized that I ended way too many conversations with anger, irritation, and frustration. And then I felt like a heel and an uncaring daughter. It was bad enough that life was interrupted and sleep was interrupted. On top of all that, I dealt with guilt and shame.

But I learned something important while taking care of Mama. Something worth sharing.

Two weeks after Mama moved into her brand-new living suite in our home, Randy and I were both gone for the afternoon. While we were away, Mama fell and fractured her back. She adjusted pretty well to the wheelchair, but the amount of attention she needed increased about a thousand percent! Before long, I was out of patience, understanding, and kindness. Her never-ending demand for my attention was taking its toll on me, on my marriage, and on my career.

After Mass one Sunday morning, as our beloved Monsignor blessed me, I told him that I needed him to pray that I would develop more patience with my mother. As a scholar of language, he replied that the Latin root words for patience mean *to suffer*. I laughingly told him I was there! I had suffered indeed!

Monsignor suggested that I use a principle that guided his life with people who challenge his patience. Very gently, as he took my hands in his, he said, "Avoid unnecessary criticism and correction."

It sounded so simple, but it was very profound. During the ensuing months, I worked purposefully to apply this ideal. Consequently, I was blessed with a closer and deeper relationship with Mama during the final months of her life. It was good advice.

An added bonus of Monsignor's lesson is that the same message works well with spouses, children, and friends.

Aunt Gladys was right. Getting old is hell! It can be a nightmare for those who care for loved ones as they age. It can be painful for those who experience deterioration of not only their bodies, but also their minds. But getting older can be a rich experience. For me, Mama's aging was a time to really learn patience and understanding. For Mama and me, it was a time for coming together, a time for compassion, and most importantly, a time for accepting life's challenges and changes. Her getting old was a little bit of Heaven — and just a little bit of Hell.

The Mother Load

The last good night's sleep I had was in 1974.

I had just moved into my very own apartment, and for the first time in my life, I was living by myself! I was a junior high school physical education teacher in the Albuquerque City Schools and thought I was on the road to a great future! I was proud of myself.

My brand-new box springs and mattress set had just been delivered. They sat atop a very old iron bedstead I had found off the side of a ranch road in southern New Mexico. I busily furnished the apartment to reflect my very eclectic style. My taste vacillated between being a free spirit of the '70s and my mother's more traditional influence. I used a quilt as a bedspread, lined my kitchen cabinets with Contact Paper, acquired matching dishes (stoneware with avocado green, orange, and gold flowers), rummaged around yard sales for antique cooking utensils and wooden spoons, displayed family pictures in brass frames, and used old wooden onion boxes for end tables and an antique trunk as a coffee table. I had matching sets of sheets and towels.

I'd been in the apartment only a week, had just celebrated my twenty-third birthday, and had started my second year teaching school. I thought to myself, "I have life by the tail!" The weather was still warm, and my teaching outfit consisted of shorts, topped by T-shirts from my latest adventure (cross-country driving and camping with my college friend, Alan). I sported the newest tennis shoes on the market—a brand called Nike—made of nylon with a red "swoosh" on the side.

Weekend outfits consisted of even less. Shorter shorts and halter-tops and always the Nike shoes. It was the '70s. I wore halter-tops that tied around the neck and in the back, barely a triangle covering my front. They were made from Indian print cotton, leather, double knit, or chamois cloth. Weekend shorts were cut-off jeans or overalls. My purse was made out of a pair of jeans—legs cut off and sewn closed across the bottom with overall suspenders for straps, and lined with country blue floral fabric.

My "Sunday" clothes (as I'd always referred to dressy outfits) were just what a mother would want her daughter to have—only too short!

Weekends were exclamation points after getting through the teaching week. My friends and I loaded Jeeps with ice chests filled with drinks and munchies and our backpacks ready for hiking and camping. Our motto was, "Look out, mountains (or the beaches of Mexico on long weekends), here we come!"

This sort of experience was new to me. I was a southern girl with a mama and daddy who dreamed of my marrying a Southern Baptist preacher. Instead, I was hiking until dusk—always on the lookout for the best sunset ever—navigating the riverbank for cooking and drinking water. We assembled our tents by starlight and moonlight, and hung a lantern inside. The flame caused the tent to glow in the dark, looking like a spaceship had landed while our backs were turned.

I had no thoughts of tomorrow—no thoughts about life back in rural Georgia where Daddy had just retired from his career as a high school principal and Mama was finishing out a couple of years until she could retire. *Then*, they said, they were going to capture the good life. They were finally going to travel around the USA! We had always gone to Daytona Beach for our family vacations. We kids loved the ocean and the sun gave Daddy months of relief from his arthritis pain. Mama was deathly afraid of the water and her skin was so fair that she sat all day in the shade just watching—and she *still* got a sunburn!

Daddy promised that when they retired, he would go anywhere she wanted to go. I knew exactly how they would do it too. They would travel by car, about 400 miles a day, then pull into a Holiday Inn or Ho Jo's. All day long they would read license plates and keep a steady eye on the fuel level and the road map. Mama would warn Daddy of a State Patrol parked by the side of the road and he would drop the speed at least fifteen miles an hour (even though he barely exceeded the speed limit). They would take turns driving. Daddy always drove first because Mama didn't awaken until about two hours after getting dressed. When she began chattering and warning Daddy of the speed limit, Daddy would know it was time for breakfast and her turn at the wheel.

Before the big trip could happen, life changed. And before I finished decorating my apartment, I received the first of many calls I would get from Mama over the next twenty-six years. It was about eleven o'clock in the evening. In a broken voice, Mama told me to get home as soon as I could. Daddy had just been diagnosed with a cerebral hemorrhage and the prognosis was not good at all—he was not conscious and was not expected to live. Looking for comfort and direction, I phoned my boyfriend and then other members of my family. I also called a teacher who had taken me under her wing (I didn't know the word *mentor* at the time). She consoled me and then made arrangements for me catch a flight to Atlanta the next morning. (Come to think of it, I never knew what the ticket cost). After a sleepless night, I numbly boarded the plane, changed aircraft in Dallas, Texas, and prayed and promised God all sorts of things. Mama's sister, Aunt Gladys, picked me up at the airport and we began the twenty-minute ride to the hospital in downtown Atlanta. I was praying so hard that Daddy would still be alive when I got there.

Miraculously, Daddy got better, but by no means well. In a few weeks, he was ready to go home from the hospital.

What happened next just happened. I don't remember any big discussions about it. I went back to Albuquerque, asked for and was granted a leave of absence from teaching, moved out of my apartment, and went back home to "look after Daddy"—just until he could manage on his own. Mama went to school each day. Her retirement was too close for her to quit teaching.

Before I left Albuquerque, the teachers gave me a farewell party, even though I was returning in four months. I loaded up my Spitfire convertible and headed home. Tucked inside my blue-jean purse were dollar bills off a "money tree" that the teachers gave me at the party, along with phone numbers and addresses of everyone who meant anything to me at that time. Eight-track tapes of Willie and Waylon and the Eagles took me farther and farther away from southwestern landscapes and midnights around the campfire. Darkness just kind of drifted in as I drove across Interstate 40. Trees blocked the star-filled nights—no sunset fanfare. And as I got closer to Georgia, I replaced my halter-top and shorts with a sweatshirt and a pair of embroidered blue jeans.

So I went home to Georgia.

Daddy got better, and I took care of him. Weekends seemed to drag out longer than the weekdays, and I started wearing my dresses just a bit longer to the Cassville Baptist Church. I shamelessly and humbly wore the crown of a loving and caring daughter who had *done the right thing* and come home to help her family. What I didn't tell anyone was that it was easier to come home than to feel the guilt I would have felt if I had abandoned my fretting mama.

At night, I slept in the same room as Daddy. The very first night I was home, Daddy climbed off the end of the hospital bed. I didn't hear him until he fell in the hallway on the way to the bathroom. After that episode I was so afraid that he would injure himself on my watch, I put aluminum pans at the bottom of the bed and on the floor so I could hear them rattle if he got up. I never heard any noise from those pans. Instead, I slept very lightly, listening for him to twist and turn. When he was better, he told people that, no matter what time of night it was, if he rolled over to face the bed where I slept, my eyes would be wide open looking at him, and I would ask "Daddy, are you okay?"

After four months, Daddy was well enough to take care of himself while Mama was at school. Much to my parents' disappointment, I went back to Albuquerque to pick up where my life had left off. I resumed my career as a teacher on weekdays and mountain girl on weekends. And each time the phone rang, I heard pain, fear, and despair in Mama's voice. My sleep was never sound, because I waited for the phone to bring me the inevitable news.

I never received the really *bad* news, but each conversation was strained. Mama just had more to deal with than she could handle. Daddy's pain was increasing. His recovery was decreasing. I hated those phone calls. I felt guilty, self-centered, and ungrateful. And often angry and frustrated.

So I went home to Georgia during summer vacation, then returned to New Mexico for the school year. Going home was hard, but not going home was harder.

And finally, after three years, I decided to stay home in Georgia. "Just for a year," I said.

Mama and Daddy moved from rural Georgia to the pleasant college community of Carrollton, Georgia, where they had family roots. This time I would teach school, and Mama would be the caretaker. This time I would leave every holiday and long weekend to get out of town and head back to the west where I knew I belonged.

As the end of the first year approached, I could tell that Mama and Daddy were holding their breaths about my decision to return to New Mexico permanently. Their needs were so great and my plans for life seemed so insignificant compared to theirs. So I decided to stay in Georgia—just one more year. Daddy's health continued to fail and they finally quit talking about traveling when he got better. It was clear that he was not going to.

I struggled with the desire in my heart to stay and the desire in my heart to leave. It wasn't easy living so close to home. Mama and I just didn't agree on very many things. I didn't think she appreciated or understood my energy and my zest for life. I couldn't understand her rigidity and need for routine. She couldn't understand how I could take things so lightly. I couldn't understand why she had become so serious, unlike the mama of my youth. She considered me frivolous. I considered her stuffy and old-fashioned.

But finally, I knew I would stay. Nothing but a memory of incredible sunsets and potential romance were waiting for me out west.

Daddy lived another sixteen years, so Mama took care of Daddy. And I took care of Mama.

After Martha Jean and I moved into our farmhouse, the phone would ring in the middle of the night and I would drive like crazy to town to help lift Daddy off the floor or to sit in the hospital emergency room, worrying with Mama. During my brief marriage to Richard, Mama *tried* not to call too many times, but she did. After that marriage ended, I spent two to three nights a week with Mama and Daddy, giving Mama a break from the constant care-giving routine.

Just about the time I married Randy, Daddy became completely bedridden. With broken hearts, we moved him into a nursing home—up to that time, the hardest move I had ever had to make. Mama visited with him three times a day to read to him, to feed him, and to just hold his hand. She refused to travel, even to visit her beloved grandchildren. She was a loyal and attentive wife every day. She was Daddy's advocate for the very best medical treatment available. She was his nurse, his friend, and most of all, his doting companion and loyal wife. Daddy died in 1995, and a part of Mama died, too.

After a while, Mama became more active in life and wanted to travel. The first trip she took was with her brother, Lloyd, and his wife, Barbara, to Daytona Beach for one last time. She came home with renewed memories of a healthy husband—and a sunburn.

I invited Mama to travel with me to some of my speaking engagements. She only went with me when the event was within driving distance—she was afraid of flying. Of course, she thought I drove too fast and, didn't buy gas nearly early enough, and she kept up an ongoing commentary about the license plates of the cars we passed. But when it came down to it, she was my biggest fan.

When we traveled, we stayed at Holiday Inns and usually ate at Wendy's or Cracker Barrel. We just didn't have the heart for ice cream at HoJo's.

In 1998, Randy and I added a bedroom suite to our house. We needed more space and we wanted to be prepared for the day Mama might need some extra care or attention. She moved in before the paint on the walls was dry. She loved to call her friends between *The Price Is Right* and *Wheel of Fortune* to brag about how wonderful life was at Randy and Shirley's. She drove her silver car (it matched her hair) to the beauty parlor for a wash and set on Friday afternoons. On Sundays, she was off to Sunday School and church. She met her friends for breakfast at Jerry's Country Kitchen and shopped for the perfect cards to take to her birthday club. Her routine was an enjoyable one, and one she reveled in.

And then, within six weeks of moving in, she fell and broke her back. It wasn't too serious—a compression fracture. But it meant a wheelchair and no more driving. She managed in her suite just fine—for a few weeks.

Bur then she got sick. Her mind became fuzzy. She couldn't prepare the meals I left for her when I had to be gone. She couldn't operate her microwave, or the remote control, or remember where her pocketbook was. She would call my office (only twelve feet down the hall) up to thirty times a day to make sure I was still home, or to ask if I knew where her pocketbook was, or to see if she could remember my office telephone number. Life got a little crazy for me.

I spent a lot of time taking Mama to the Doctor's office, looking for her pocketbook, and reassuring her that I was in my office just down the hall.

So, on another very sad day, Mary and I moved Mama into the Stewart House, a beautiful and nurturing assisted-living home. She was confused about being moved. She couldn't understand that she required full-time assistance—something that didn't work with my speaking schedule. She was like a child being left behind. She called me on the telephone all day long again, to tell me that her pocketbook was missing or to just make sure she could remember my telephone number. Life was getting a little crazy for her too.

And then one day she couldn't remember my telephone number or even remember what a pocketbook was. I knew she was very sick. She was sicker than Daddy had been up until he died. So I brought her home. Back to *her* suite. Back to *her* bedroom. Bedridden, semiconscious, but comfortable in the hospital bed in her room. She didn't know very much during those last few weeks. She only knew that she was at home and that I was very close by, practicing patience and being her biggest fan and advocate.

During the day, two special caregivers took care of her every need, so I could spend time just holding her hand and soothing her. At night, I slept lightly so I could hear her call out over the baby monitor that connected our rooms. Within a few weeks, she died—on the same date as her only sister, Aunt Gladys.

She was a mother load. And in the midst of the load, I

discovered a mother lode.

Life has a way of putting you right where you need to be when you need to be there.

Filling Up Heart Spaces

One summer afternoon, Zeke, my oldest grandson, was standing in front of the glass door just staring out. It was the perfect opportunity to sneak in a hug. I walked up behind him, put my arms over his shoulders, and pulled him close to me. He nestled back against me, relaxed, and sighed in comfort. After a few seconds of snuggling, he tilted his head up toward mine and said, "Gran-Gran, did you know that when certain people hug you, it fills up your heart a certain number of spaces?"

Momentarily overcome with the beauty of that thought, I remained still and enjoyed our special time together.

Later that evening, I asked him, "Zeke, just how many spaces are in your heart?" Without skipping a beat, he replied, "Ten," and then he continued, "But, Gran-Gran, if you want to feel really good, at least seven spaces have to be filled."

I have thought about that a lot and have quoted Zeke many times since that summer afternoon, too. I don't believe there is any gift in the world greater than filling up heart spaces.

I believe from the bottom of my heart that people with full

heart spaces do not shoot people and they do not drive airplanes into buildings. They do not abuse their spouses, their children or their pets. I believe that people with full heart spaces are not violent, they don't yell, and they don't honk their horns at you just as the light turns green.

And I also know that we come into contact every day with people who have empty heart spaces. We live with them. We work with them. We do business with them. And sometimes we ARE them.

Of all the jobs we have on this earth, I feel that filling each other's heart spaces might be the most important one. Of course, we can't physically hug each person we see (not in this litigious society), but we can give hugs in other ways. Maybe it's through a smile. Or by looking someone in the eye and saying, "Thank you." Or perhaps it could be by *really* listening with our hearts to another person. Maybe doing our job the best we can will fill up someone's heart. Or maybe hearts are filled when we give our time to a person or a cause. Or maybe, just maybe, heart spaces are filled when we simply look another human being in the eye and, with our soul, say, "I care."

I believe that people who fill the heart spaces of others end up with a full heart themselves. And a full heart is a peaceful and kind heart. Something the world can use just a little more of.

Going Home

To A Place I've Never Been

Randy's tennis has taken on a life of its own. He retired from farming and spends his time devoted to tennis lessons, matches, teaching, and tournament play. One of the best spin-offs of tennis is the fascinating and diverse people we meet and the places we travel. In January 2002, friends invited us to join them in Europe for a tennis tournament. I couldn't believe it! I had never traveled to another continent and we were going to fly to Germany and drive to Austria for Randy to play in the European Championship Tennis Tournament. It wasn't one of his most successful tournaments, but it *was* the trip of a lifetime.

One of the most defining moments of the trip occured when I was standing outside an apartment house in Bodenmais, Germany.

I pressed the intercom button and held my breath until I heard a young, masculine "Hal-lo."

"Do you speak English?" I shouted back into the speaker.

"Hal-lo, hal-lo," he repeated.

Louder and slower this time, "Do you speak English? Is your name Wolfl?"

Seconds passed—seconds of disappointing silence changing to excitement as I heard footsteps from a staircase inside the apartment building. With my heart in my throat, I strained to get a better look at him in the light of the opening door.

"I'm an American," I haltingly said, "and I'm looking for the Wolfl family."

His eyes registered recognition as I clumsily spoke his family name. At last we had connected. The elation quickly faded when I tried to explain what I wanted. He understood no English and I spoke no German.

Remembering that louder does not guarantee comprehension, I struggled to determine how to communicate. Slowly I began, "My birth mother was named Maria Wolfl."

Questioning eyes looked back at me, now joined by the inquisitive identical eyes of his five year-old son.

I started again, "My mother."

Yes, he understood.

"Bodenmais, 1929."

Another nod of the head

I didn't know how to proceed.

Sensing mounting confusion, I shouted, "Un momento, por favor"—as if the only Spanish words I knew were going to help. I ran to the car to get paper and pencil and to let Randy know I had found someone to ask about my birth mother.

I stood on the apartment stoop and began drawing. Stick figure for father—stick figure for mother. Wedding bells with the date 1948. I pointed to the male saying, "American," and the female saying, "Bodenmais." So far he was with me. A quickly sketched outline of the United States with arrows pointing toward the country let him know that Maria Wolfl and her husband had left Germany.

"Baby," I said, as I made the universal sign of a mother rocking a baby in her arms. And then I drew 1- 2- 3- 4 stick children. As I pointed to the third child and back to myself, I knew he was figuring it out.

Now, how to tell him the rest of the story? How do I explain that my birth mother, this elusive Maria Wolfl, had left her four children in an orphanage? Pulling a tiny, yellow German dictionary from my coat pocket, leaning into the light of the foyer, I looked up the word *orphan*. Circling the German word, *waise* I handed the dictionary to him.

As I pointed to the words and then to the four stick children, I could sense that the pieces of the puzzle were coming together for him. I noticed his eyes glance toward his own son as if to try to comprehend how any parent could leave a child.

Suddenly he stirred and appeared to be on a mission. Somehow I began to understand that his parents, older Wolfls, lived next door and we should go and ask them if they knew of a Maria Wolfl.

The walk was only about 100 feet, but my anticipation grew every step of the way.

"Am I about to meet an aunt or uncle?" I asked myself. "Or maybe a cousin?"

"Will a grandparent be living in the home? Am I finally going to connect with the most mysterious part of my life?"

"Will someone open the door and see Maria Wolfl's face in my face and collapse in uncontrollable joy at finally meeting her daughter?"

As we entered his parents' home, I was suddenly shy. Hanging back, I waited while this young man—whose name I did not even know—began to share my life story. Confusion, then interest, and then a little shock registered on his parents' faces.

Before I saw the shake of their heads, I could sense that they had never heard of a Maria Wolfl.

But now they were part of the puzzle. The father began talking earnestly and eagerly to the mother. Suddenly her eyes lit up with an idea. She excused herself to the next room, and I heard her dialing the telephone and rapidly and excitingly telling the story.

When she came back, the look on her face was enough for me to know that she had nothing to report. I knew she, too, was disappointed. After more conversation with her husband and son, she left the room again . . . only to return with the same look of defeat on her face. After two or three more "takes" of this scene, I decided that we all had tried hard enough. It was time to let go. These generous people had done more than enough to help me attempt to solve the riddle.

I thanked everyone profusely and Randy gave the little boy some Euro coins to play with. It was all we really had to give back.

The son used the dictionary and pencil and paper to explain that there would be records of Maria Wolfl at the registrar's office in the village. He suggested we go there the next morning.

As we got into the car to begin our four-hour journey back to Austria, I could tell that Randy was cautious as he asked me how I felt. Was being here so close, and trying so hard, enough? I knew he was afraid I would be disappointed—let down.

Searching deep inside my heart and my soul, I knew this was enough for right now.

We were on a last-minute trip to Austria, and I never

dreamed we would even be able to find Bodenmais, Germany. I'd been looking on maps for years and had never found the town. When we finally met someone who could direct us to the obscure village on the eastern border of Germany, deep in the Bavarian Forest, I never thought we would have an unexpected day on our agenda to be able to go. Never had I ever imagined we would locate people named Wolfl.

As I watched the village fade from the rearview mirror, I knew something new. Sometimes in life we get answers to our questions and sometimes we don't. But it is the search that teaches us what we need to know.

And I know that somehow, even if it is a continent and a language away, we will always find people who want to help right the world for us.

And that is enough.

Epilogue

Tree Houses and Tomato Sandwiches

I'm sitting in my favorite spot in the world—the screened-in porch at home. It overlooks the crystal clear water of our cove on the lake, and I have a bird's-eye view of the bass swimming near our dock. Squirrels jump from tree to tree, chasing each other like kids playing kick-the-can in Center Lot. Someone across the lake is cutting grass, the whir of the motor blending nicely with the steady noise from our ceiling fan. It's a hot, humid day here in Georgia and I'm grateful for the steady breeze.

My laptop computer is hooked up to extension cords so I can sit out here to finish my writing. But before I started writing, I just had to have a tomato sandwich, southern style. Yesterday I stopped at a house nearby to buy tomatoes. No one was home, so I followed the hand-written instructions on a paper sack, held in place with a rock. I left a couple of one-dollar bills in the paper cup (also weighted down with a rock) and just as I was about to leave, decided to add another three dollars for some Georgia peaches. They were just like the ones Daddy and Mr. Williamson used to buy by the truckload in South Georgia. I knew they would be perfectly ripe in time for today's lunch.

A tomato sandwich is a southern delicacy. One that most true Southerners never outgrow. Several years ago, Randy and I were visiting our friends, Russ and Louise Goldsmith, at their summer place in Lake Tahoe. They are from New York City and fascinated us with tales of big-city life. We couldn't begin to imagine life without a car, but they only had one when they were at Lake Tahoe. When at home in New York, they took taxis or had drivers on call. That amazed us.

During one summer visit at Lake Tahoe, Randy was off playing tennis and I began thinking about fixing his lunch. Spotting a luscious red tomato, I told Russ that I thought Randy would love a tomato sandwich and asked if I could fix him one too. Russ asked, "Tomatoes and what else?"

I replied, "Some mayonnaise and maybe a little salt and pepper."

Russ repeated himself, "What else?"

I thought to myself that he must want the entire menu. So I replied, "Maybe some chips and a glass of ice-cold milk."

"No," Russ insisted, "what else on the sandwich?"

Exasperated at this point, I said, "Russ, *it's a tomato sandwich!* Two pieces of soft white bread, mayonnaise, maybe some salt and pepper. That's it. A tomato sandwich!"

Russ shook his head in disbelief and declined. When Randy got home, he ate two sandwiches and washed them down with two glasses of ice-cold milk.

Later Russ confessed to me that, when we weren't looking, he went into the kitchen and made a tomato sandwich. He said it wasn't too bad, just a little boring. I think he was used to New York City kind of sandwiches—the kind with lots of stuff on them.

Anyway, I've just finished my own tomato sandwich and am loving the chance to sit on the porch. It's on the second floor of the house and so close to the trees that I can touch several from the deck beside the screened porch. I love being so high up in the trees. I feel like I'm in a tree house, something I've wanted all my life.

My first tree-climbing experiences were in the big house in Butler. By the time I was six years old, I'd discovered the secret hiding places in trees. When we went to visit Grandmother Gillham, I would hide underneath the skirt of the magnificent magnolia trees, climb the lower branches, and pretend I was in fairyland. When I was nine, I rode my bike to a friend's house to climb the sturdy branches of a chinaberry tree and hold secret club meetings.

I just knew that, someday, I was going to have my own tree house.

After turning eleven, I finished the Bobsey Twins series, and realized that the other fictional heroine, Nancy Drew, lived a life vastly different from mine. I began searching the library for novels about girls like me. One day I found a book that spoke to my spirit. The title was *Best Friends*, and the book was about a girl who had her very own tree house. The heroine (I can't believe that I can't remember her name!) spent a lot of time in the tree house trying to figure things out. The tree house was fabulous, equipped with a pulley and bucket that went up and down with food and secret messages.

The book was a great story about best friends, romance, and most of all, the special delights of a tree house. I read and reread that book until I could draw the tree house in my sleep.

This back porch of our home is my version of a tree house. Here I sit and listen to the sounds of nature. I have watched grandchildren and other children jump off the dock and explore life. I have talked countless hours on the phone, listening to family gossip, sharing the challenges of the speaking profession with colleagues, or just laughing and reconnecting with old friends.

It is on this back porch that I started journaling and meditating. And it is here that I lift up my greatest needs and concerns to God in prayer. I've read novels, magazines, professional journals, and the comics on this back porch. I have cried a few tears, argued with myself, and made resolutions in my tree house. I have entertained friends and served country-fried steak, banana pudding, and homemade ice cream among the tree branches. I have watched lightning bugs dance on a summer's eve and listened to the tunes of pop-up thunderstorms and rain on the tin roof.

It is here that I have crystallized some of the life lessons in this book. In my very own version of a tree house, I have been able to come to terms with who I am—a woman with a spirit that can be too boisterous, shoulders and feet that are too broad, and a voice that is not melodic enough.

I've also figured out that most of the events in my life just happened. I realize that, as a child or a naïve young woman, I didn't have the power or the wisdom to change much about the hand life dealt me. But more importantly, I realize that the choices I have made and the lessons I have learned because of those events make me uniquely me. I like that and I like some of the lessons.

Lessons like God created step-daddies, and every kid needs a Butler. I have learned that every heart has ten spaces, that the best eggs are scrambled with love, and that *all* voices are melodic enough. Through the years, I've discovered that courage is like a muscle and the more you exercise it, the more you have. I believe that you can see God on a starry, starry night if you want to. And I know that I am a tap water girl in a bottled water world.

That's what this book has been about. Finding comfort in who we are. Finding the fit, and realizing that we all fit. Sure, the stories have been told through the voice of an orphaned child, a southern girl, and an evolving woman. But the story of belonging and becoming is universal. And these reflections have helped me discover what really matters.

As you read these stories, I hope you saw how you fit into your world and that you embraced the feeling of belonging. As you continue to look at your own experiences, I hope memories of a delightful life emerge. Memories of love, learning, laughing, and a soaring spirit. And, I hope that you have discovered what really matters to you.

Acknowledgments

For months, I have tried to figure out a way to say thank you to the many, many people who have encouraged me to complete this book. And then I realized, that is a whole other book. But there are some incredibly special friends who have made my life richer. Their presence in my life keeps my heart spaces full. A special thanks to:

Martha Jean and Jimmy Smith. You made the dream come true. Thanks for sharing more than the journey. I love you.

The BKB's: Julie Alexander, Barb Wingfield, and Robin Thompson. You changed the way I see myself and the future.

Fred Richards. If the world could experience your lust for life, quest for honesty, and belief in the human spirit, it would indeed be heaven on earth. You helped me become the adult I needed to meet as a four year-old.

Cousin Dorothy Jean, you were relentless in your belief that there was a book in me. Thanks for the gentle nudging.

Sam Horn, the best writing coach in the world. You gave me the courage to trust my message.

Levi, Zeke, Hayley, and Nala Garrett, and Janie Brooke and Brent Worsham for begging me to do cart wheels off the dock into the lake. You keep me young!

Chris Clarke Epstein for giving me the tools, the inspiration, and the encouragement to be a writer. You are a terrific teacher, mentor, and friend.

Mark LeBlanc for teaching me how to run a business (at least you keep trying to!) and for being my number one advocate!

Graphic designers Patti Barrett and Linda Winsbro for discovering the essence of the book.

My "speaking" friends who make this profession the best in the world: Kathy Dempsey, Jane Riley, June Cline, Glenna Salsbury, Karen Rowinsky, Marilynn Mobley, and Marcia Steele.

The Camp Garrett — Great American Kid's Camp kids who remind me to approach life with enthusiasm and a jump off the high dock: Lizzie, Susan, Kristen, Emily, Levi, Brent, Stephen, Michael, and Zeke.

My girlfriends: Dori, Brenda, Kelly, Helen, Martha, Sonia, Annette, Pam, Myra, and Karen. You celebrate all my funny stories, encourage me to tell more, and make me giggle.

My courageous friend Retha. You are my role model. Because of you nad Marcia, I walked in faith.

Three very special girlfriends who make me laugh, wipe my tears, and know when to tell me what I want to hear and when to tell me what I need to hear: Wendy Almon, you are an angel walking among us; Kitty Cleghorn, you always find the silver lining and have shown it to me countless time; and Suzanne Worsham, you are my anchor and my walking, talking, and listening friend. No matter what is going on, I know that one (or all three of you) can help me figure it out.

My *readers* whose insights took this book to another level: Ann Ball, Lynn Marquardt, Linda Harvey, Kay Makarenko, Dorothy Jean, Louise Gentry, Wendy Almon, and Kay duPont.

My college friend and life friend, Alan Speaker. You have wanted the best for me for a very long time and helped me discover the best. And to Linda Speaker for sharing your family and yourself.

Miriam Phillips for jump starting the book with insightful proof reading.

My agent, Roger Jellinek. For believing that *Tap Water Girl* is going places!

Margaret and Handley Boone for becoming my next set of parents.

Marsha Sullins Lee. You were my first real best friend. You taught me to laugh at life's foibles, you encouraged my mischievous spirit, and most of all, you kept telling me to just be myself — something that took me a long time to learn.

My husband, Randy, even though you haven't always understood what I do, you've helped make it happen. Thanks for believing in me. And I really, really love the tree house you gave me. You are my *dumpling*.

Finally, my sister Mary. I have loved you your entire life. The joys in life have multiplied because of you and the inevitable pain has more than halved. Thank you for being more than just my sister, thanks for being my best friend.

Reflections on Belonging and Believing

Capture your own tap water experiences. Use the following blank pages to jot down:

- Highlights of your life's journey.

- People who held your hand and gave you a boost.

- Memories that fill up your heart spaces.

- Lessons learned — the hard way and the easy way.

Reflections on Belonging and Believing

REFLECTIONS ON BELONGING AND BELIEVING

REFLECTIONS ON BELONGING AND BELIEVING

REFLECTIONS ON BELONGING AND BELIEVING

Contact Shirley!

Shirley would love to hear from you. You may contact her at drshirl@tapwatergirl.com or visit her web site, www.tapwatergirl.com.

There you will find a photo gallery including pictures of Aunt Audie, the boys, the Cassville Post Office, and the Camp Garrett kids.

Additionally, you can find the answer to questions you may have after reading this book, such as: Has Shirley kept in touch with her birth brothers? Or, why is a Southern Baptist girl talking with a Catholic Priest?

If you have a tap-water story, a story of discovering what really matters, send it to Shirley. And receive Shirley's monthly e-mail tips by signing up on-line.

Books clubs are encouraged to send for a copy of book club discussion questions. Shirley will be happy to discuss the possibility of speaking to your book club when she is in your area.

You may write Shirley at:

1317 Forest Court
Villa Rica, GA 30180

Three easy ways to order additional
copies of this book:

Phone: (770) 836-1926
E-Mail: drshirl@tapwatergirl.com
Web Site: www.tapwatergirl.com

About the Author

Shirley Garrett is a professional speaker, writer, and facilitator. When she was a little girl she couldn't decide if she wanted to grow up to be Lucille Ball or Miss America. She did neither. But what she did grow up to be is a woman who is clear about the importance of appreciating the life God gave her.

Shirley holds a Doctorate degree and is affectionately known to her friends as Dr. Shirl. She works with organizations that want to create a new sense of spirit in the workplace and community and with people who want to re-discover what is really important in life.

Shirley lives in Villa Rica, Georgia, with her husband Randy. She opens her home to family and friends and her heart to the world.